PRAISE FOR *THE FEAR...*
GUIDE TO STARTING A BUSINESS

"As a therapist, as a fellow female entrepreneur, I want to shout from the rooftops about HOW IMPORTANT this book is! What hardly anyone tells you is that going into business for yourself necessitates some real personal growth work, which causes so many people to give up before they've shared their greatness with the world. With this witty, engaging book, packed full of relatable metaphors and information about how we're affected by stress, Ameé provides vitally necessary information to help women succeed. I truly wish I had this book when I started my business; it would've deeply empowered me from the start."

—**Sarah A Gilbert**, LCSW, Transitions Therapy LLC

"Ameé is an incredibly impressive human! She is brilliant, for starters. She is also multidimensionally talented, curious, and fiercely committed to helping others in their quest for growth and transformation. Ameé can articulate a thought, an idea, a proposal, theory...with so much clarity, genuineness, experience, and thoughtfulness."

—**Wendy Behary**, author of *Disarming the Narcissist: Surviving and Thriving with the Self-Absorbed* and clinical and training director at The Schema Therapy Institute of NJ-NYC-DC

"Ameé covers everything womxn need to know about having a huge impact on the world with their businesses—from confidence, to making money, handling haters, and living your values and integrity. This is the book I wish I'd had five years ago. If you want to be unstoppable while creating a sustainable business, this is a must read."

—Melanie Childers, master coach for feminist entrepreneurs

"Ameé Quiriconi's book is a guide for smart, ambitious women who want to make their mark on the world with confidence. She walks you through a practical step-by-step journey to shifting your mindset and calling on your own resilience and resourcefulness."

—Rachel Beider, bestselling author of *Massage MBA: Run Your Practice, Love Your Life* and globally recognized small business expert

"Ameé Quiriconi is blazing a trail for others who may feel 'stuck' in a holding pattern of personal development. Her works are must reads!"

—Sharon St. Marie, owner of The Belle Chapel

"Ameé has a true and deep understanding of what it is to free oneself from the internal and external systems that oppress and suppress women like us. I recommend this book for any woman with an entrepreneurial spirit, women who lead, and those that love women who seek to find their truth."

—Shannon Ivey, MFA AEA, founder and creative fairy godmother of #whatshesaidproject

"Reading this book is like sitting with your best friend and sharing bits of wisdom over coffee or tea. Ameé writes in a very refreshing and genuine way. Her guide is an eye-opener, hear-opener, mind-opener! I would recommend it to anyone wanting to move in the right direction in life and business."

—**Michaella Rugwizangoga**, business leader, poet, member of the World Economic Forum Future Global Council on Mobility

"I have always referred Ameé as a coach when I know an entrepreneur is struggling—and not because their business plan is weak, but because Ameé knows how to get straight to the heart of challenging issues that foil otherwise great execution. If you need help getting out of your own way, then follow Ameé's advice."

—**Wendy Poischbeg**, economic development director and entrepreneurship blogger

"In *The Fearless Woman's Guide to Starting a Business*, Ameé offers an inspiring playbook for women who are passionate about caging their fears and crushing their entrepreneurial goals."

—**Dr. Brad Klontz**, financial psychologist and author of *Money Mammoth: Harness the Power of Financial Psychology to Evolve Your Money Mindset, Avoid Extinction, and Crush Your Financial Goals*

"This book is written with every intention of supplying ALL women the knowledge to reflect, understand, pursue, and implement the necessities to create a phenomenal business and a true sense of self. A page-turner with smiles and agreeance throughout, this book is one that EVERY woman should read, before and during any stage of entrepreneurship."

—**Irene Wilkins**, cofounder and chief solutionist at Achievet Business Solutions, LLC

"This book calls out why we crave validation from others and strips that toxic narrative down to its core. The reader feels unsure, even unsafe in the beginning, then empowered, and ultimately walks away with a deep knowing and self-awareness every human being should have. It's a must-read for all women, femmes, and underdogs—not just entrepreneurs."

—**Maggie Greene**, CEO of Maggie Greene Style

"I wish that Ameé's book, *The Fearless Woman's Guide to Starting a Business*, was written sooner! When I started my business as a single mom just getting out of a DV relationship, I didn't have that blueprint that Ameé outlines in her guide, so I floundered a LOT longer than I needed to. I also appreciated that she also explained how trauma and sexism can prevent us from really going after what we want (and deserve!). Even though I've been running my business since 2008, I found that her chapter on finding value and changing my money mindset was exactly what I needed to hear to begin to take my earnings to the next level."

—**Giovannie Espiritu**, founder of HollywoodActorsWorkshop. com

"Ameé forges a path between your childhood experiences and family dynamics to give you practical advice on how to best approach entrepreneurship. Her book is helpful in understanding where you came from and how that can effectively get you where you're going on your career journey. I found it insightful, well-written, and sensible."

—Ariel Kochbarski, fashion and creative consultant at Of The Momnt

"Ameé gets it! It's so much more than a guide to starting a business, it is a guide for succeeding while living your best life. For the more than 80 percent of woman who were raised in dysfunction, the information packed in these pages will help you channel that experience into a superpower. *The Fearless Woman's Guide to Starting a Business* bridges that gap between dysfunction and trauma, how this plays out in our professional lives, and what to do about it before it sabotages you."

—Lara Currie, author of *Difficult Happens: How Triggers Boundaries & Emotions Impact You Every Day*

"Most aspiring business owners will ask questions like 'How do I start a business?' and 'What are the steps?' While these are important questions, their answers never address the nuance, the complexities, and the difficulties behind taking these steps. That's why what I love about this book is that it is not a how-to of what to do; rather it's a how-to of how to be. Ameé takes us on a journey and reveals reasons behind our actions and beliefs (and the why under the why) that allow us to truly move forward in a way that will allow us to be more successful than we've ever dreamed in our businesses, careers, and lives."

—Sharon Podobnik Peterson, founder and head leadership coach at The Center for Conscious Leadership

"If you're looking for a utilitarian book about starting a business, Ameé Quirconi's *The Fearless Woman's Guide to Starting a Business* is not for you. She doesn't talk about writing business plans or setting up websites, but instead delves into the psychology and mindset needed to be a successful entrepreneur. I wish I had had this book twenty years ago when I started my business."

—Molly Gimmel, CEO of Design To Delivery, Inc. and past chair of NAWBO

"Blending concepts in neuroscience, business wisdom, and personal, hard-earned life lessons, Ameé's writing is at once relatable, fascinating, and invigorating. As a woman, marketer, and aspiring social entrepreneur, I deeply resonate with the chapter on authenticity and integrity. And I'm sure you too will find those moments of 'yes!' that I did. The icing on the cake are the powerful exercises that Ameé integrates throughout to help you personalize the concepts. Bravo, Ameé!"

—Katherine Lewis, MBA, senior manager in technology innovation and aspiring entrepreneur

The Fearless Woman's Guide to Starting a Business

The Fearless Woman's Guide to Starting a Business

What Every Woman Needs to Know to Be a Courageous, Authentic and Unstoppable Entrepreneur

AMEÉ QUIRICONI

mango
PUBLISHING GROUP

Coral Gables

For permission requests, please contact the publisher at:

Mango Publishing Group
2850 Douglas Road, 2nd Floor
Coral Gables, FL 33134 USA
info@mango.bz

For special orders, quantity sales, course adoptions and corporate sales, please email the publisher at sales@mango.bz. For trade and wholesale sales, please contact Ingram Publisher Services at customer.service@ingramcontent.com or +1.800.509.4887.

The Fearless Woman's Guide to Starting a Business: What Every Woman Needs to Know to Be a Courageous, Authentic, and Unstoppable Entrepreneur

ISBN: (p) 978-1-64250-517-7 (e) 978-1-64250-518-4

BISAC: BUS109000, BUSINESS & ECONOMICS / Women in Business

LCCN: 2021931721

Printed in the United States of America.

This book is for my kids, Oz and Reese:

I want you guys to see that anyone can overcome their shitty childhoods and reclaim their future, even you.

And to Brian, the Merlin to my King Arthur.

> *"Each friend represents a world in us, a world possibly not born until they arrive, and it is only by this meeting that a new world is born."*

—*Anaïs Nin*,
The Diary of Anaïs Nin,
Vol 1: 1931-1934

TABLE OF CONTENTS

FOREWORD

I walked into my local bookstore recently and noticed that about a quarter of the shelf space was taken up with business books. I wasn't surprised—there's a reason that there is an entire category of books about building companies. A lot of people aspire to be entrepreneurs, and many of those people want a map or a checklist for how to do so successfully. Unfortunately for those that like to follow well-defined steps, there's no one right way of starting a business. The possibilities are nearly as infinite as the combinations of company missions and founder attributes. If there was a simple instruction manual, there would be far fewer books on the subject.

That's why I love the approach Ameé takes in *The Fearless Woman's Guide to Starting a Business*. Don't let the title mislead you—this book is much more about understanding and evolving yourself than it is a recipe for business processes. And that's what makes it impactful.

Before embarking on a new journey—such as that of a business owner—it's valuable to reflect back on where you've been. This is something I've done many times on my own nonlinear path, and it's also an exercise that we lead women through on OwnTrail, the company I cofounded to provide a peer-to-peer support system for women. Looking back gives us the opportunity to observe patterns in how we navigate experiences, take inventory of our internal resources, and be conscious about what behaviors and beliefs we want to carry forward with us and which ones we should leave behind.

Ameé provides insights into psychology, neuroscience, and statistics to help readers uncover where we're coming from so that we can better understand where we are headed. This approach is valuable for anyone, and particularly so for women, as our personal and professional lives are so inherently intertwined. Many business books only focus on the professional dimension of ourselves, which can really sell our experience short and overlook crucial parts of our entrepreneurial journey. As Ameé put it, "despite the desire to flip switches between your 'normal brain' and 'business brain'—it's all one brain."

While Ameé's insights into developmental neuroplasticity, gender roles in finances, and frameworks for resiliency are incredibly valuable, it's her focus on authenticity that particularly resonates with me. It takes so much mental work to conform to values or norms that are not authentic to us— mental work that could be going into building successful, innovative businesses.

When we are authentically aligned with our businesses, it keeps us going through the difficult parts and frees up mental space so that we can be more creative and productive. And, as Ameé points out, our customers notice it too: "You can't make that real connection with [your customers] unless you are real with yourself." In order to build an authentic, trustworthy brand that centers customers as people, rather

17

than commodities or sales channels, we have to be authentic and trustworthy ourselves.

The interesting thing about becoming more authentic is that it looks different for everyone. Because we have all experienced different familial and societal influences, we all have different internalized biases that can challenge our levels of authenticity. One of the exercises that **Ameé** leads readers through is based on owning stories and crafting future narratives. I love this process, which is very aligned with the way women share their trails on OwnTrail, because it's a powerful act of reflection and visualization. The way we connect the dots of our past experiences can both show us how much we have accomplished and made it through so far and help us imagine how the path that has led us here can evolve to so much more—including that of a successful business owner.

As someone who recently left my corporate executive career to start a company myself, I know how enticing the idea of a playbook can sound. Starting a business is risky and unpredictable and can leave you feeling vulnerable. I've had to learn new job functions quickly, deal with external events outside of my control, and weather countless ups and downs. But I also know that the resources that have gotten me successfully through my first year of entrepreneurship aren't ones that can be checked off a list. They are exactly the resources that **Ameé** helps readers to identify and evolve in themselves: self-awareness, vision, authenticity, resiliency, and a supportive community.

While **Ameé** doesn't sugarcoat her message, it's ultimately an optimistic one: we all have the ability to grow in the areas we need to. If you are passionate about your *why* for starting a business, **Ameé** will give you the how.

Enjoy your entrepreneurial journey—you've got this!

Rebekah Bastian
CEO and cofounder of OwnTrail
Author of *Blaze Your Own Trail*

A BOOK FOR ALL WOMXN

If this is the first page you read while deciding if you should buy this book or not, I want to be clear that this book is for all **womxn**. And words do matter.

Some of you may have arrived at this place of womxnhood through a long, hard fought battle to uncover your authentic selves by waging war against the belief systems that said your biological sex and gender were the same thing; the same rule of thought we've all been living under. A rule of thought that still exists today, as many of you know, in professional settings as well as our personal communities.

I also realize that a few of you have found yourself in a place where you have fearlessly shrugged off a gender label altogether, despite our society's ardent attempt to repeatedly stick it back on you.

And I would venture to guess that some of you are men, interested in expanding your own views of the world and your awareness of how business is different for women. Or maybe you just want to learn how to be a courageous, authentic, and unstoppable entrepreneur, in which case, this book will definitely do that for you.

In this book I am using my voice as a person raised as a **woman**, who was told how to live and behave as a woman. As you read, you will see this term repeated because, like I mentioned earlier, words do matter. Therefore, I am speaking to you as someone who has struggled to thrive, personally and professionally, with the weight of that word and its association with certain expectations, among other things, on my shoulders. And you will see in the following pages, I will share the research and evidence of how these beliefs impacted all of us and what to do to cast them away so that we can be amazing entrepreneurs.

Since there are no children reading this book, then the facts are that the mark of gender is already here in our adult lives, like fossilized footprints on our pathway. It influences us on conscious and unconscious levels. We can choose to change our future and give gender stereotypes a reduced power over us, but if we try to pretend they don't exist, we risk our footfalls echoing them back to us.

That's why it is important for me to let you know that how the world saw you when you were growing up is what I am speaking to here. And as we move together through this book, I want you to keep in mind that the beliefs our parents and cultures have about gender and how these beliefs undermine women in business is what I have put on trial for us to cross-examine. And despite how my title is worded, I am not promoting a limited view of gender that continues to marginalize and limit all womxn and our capacity to do great things together.

• • •

Introduction

GRAB A DRINK

Let me set the stage.

The scene is happy hour at a cocktail lounge and there is
a group of women sitting around on plush couches with
dim lighting, taking full advantage of half-price drinks. You
and I have never met but we have a shared friend who
invited us both to join this weekly ritual of socializing with
adult beverages.

Apparently, this group of women gets together regularly
to muse about their side hustles, bosses, coworkers, and
otherwise share their frustrations with sympathetic and
understanding ears before most of them peel off and head
home. There, many of them then assume the other roles of
mother, wife, or whatever else is always waiting for them at
the end of every day.

At some point during the conversation, the topic turns to
starting a business. Suddenly, your ears perk up because you
have been thinking about doing this for quite some time
now. You have been making handmade jewelry for years and
have often wondered if you could turn it into a full-fledged
business instead of just a hobby.

So, sensing a pause in the conversation, you take the opportunity to then speak up and ask the group, "I want to start my own business and don't know where to begin. What do you guys recommend?"

Our mutual friend pops up in her seat and says, "Oh wait—you have to hear this. This is why I asked her to come tonight." She turns to me and says, "Ameé, tell everyone your story." Our friend then nestles—rather dramatically, if you ask me—back into her seat, clutching her glass of wine, preparing herself for the long haul with a shit-eating grin because she knows what's next.

Feeling uncomfortable because I normally prefer to remain a fly on the wall and ease myself into a group of people I don't really know, here I am being singled out. I lift myself up from my hiding position I had taken on the couch, reach out to grab my margarita off the table in front of me, and take a long sip on the straw. I look around into the faces of everyone in our circle, all looking back at me and then I turn to you and ask, "Well, do you want to know the easy way or the right way?"

You look right back at me and without hesitation say, "Definitely the right way."

And just like that, you didn't know it, but you and I instantly become friends.

So, as your friend, I want to make sure that as I answer your question, I get right to the point as directly as possible. Because I don't know if I'll ever see you again, but I want to make damn sure that I make an impression on you that will leave you thinking about our conversation for a while. Because I have codes I live by and one of them is that there is no bullshit to be found in my world. You will know where I stand and the only motivation behind what I say—no matter how pointed or salty it seems—is that I really do want to see you win.

Now, before you ask, no, I have not personally turned myself into a multi-millionaire with anything I've done so far. So why is my experience even worth sharing? Well, you see, in business I've done some pretty cool things and have done them really fast. It's what makes me a good coach and teacher. I've had an instinct for many things related to business, as well as an insane curiosity to keep learning and become an expert in any field I wanted to, giving me a huge toolbox to build and create with over the years.

My journey into entrepreneurship started back in 2003. That year, I invented a countertop out of garbage, literally, that sold $500,000 a year and diverted several million tons of trash from the waste stream. Yes, I turned trash into money and sold it to supermodels and rock stars, but I lost it all eight years later. It was shortly after my marriage ended and I blamed it on the extreme pressure of the recession and many other things I will talk about later.

Right after that, I moved to the country and grew a backyard wedding business earning less than $10,000 a year into an award-winning, six-figure business in less than two years. But then I expanded it to two locations, tripled revenues, and over the next five years, it would earn nearly two million dollars in gross sales. This business went from losing money to earning stupid amounts of it.

So, I do know about starting from an idea at a kitchen table to growing a business to the multi-million-dollar level, which is why sometimes people are interested in what I have to say. But the reason my friend is so eager to sit back in her seat and listen to the stories she's already heard me tell is that I know how to do all of that and have nothing to show for it. Zero. Zilch. Nada.

Because in 2017, I lost it all again—another relationship and another business—and I just knew I couldn't blame a recession or a terrible business partner or a lousy marriage *again*. Instead, I stood in the wake of loss and saw for the first time it was all on me. I didn't know why it was, but my mathematical brain could see a pattern and that *I* was the common denominator in the rising and falling of everything I did.

Here—I had lots of verifiable successes on the business front to point to: television appearances, magazine features, famous customers, and on and on. But once it was said and done, I had nothing but a box of memories in my hands as I had to go find a new place to start over again.

I wasn't wealthy like I imagined. And I wasn't happy. I was stressed and broke and thought I was destined to never get what I wanted. I truly believed that I was cursed with too many big ideas that were never meant to be mine. That I could dream up the fantasy, turn it into money, but that I was never meant to keep it.

And that was horse shit.

That's when I sat on my couch and decided that I would use my curious and creative mind on myself for once and solve the puzzle of what was happening. And then I spent two years doing just that.

But a funny thing happened while on the journey of personal discovery—lightning struck again. About four months into this healing process, feeling an intense sense of purpose, I was compelled to share what I was learning with others, so I decided to start a podcast called *One Broken Mom*.

And in only one year, I would go from reading life-changing books to actually meeting and interviewing those very authors on my show. And several of these women and men would go from being the names on the cover of my favorite books to professional colleagues and even friends.

But after spending a couple of years immersed in the field of psychology, neuroscience, and self-help, all while continuing to coach women business owners, I began to see the natural intersection between the two more clearly. My reasons for failure were not mine alone and that's when I knew I needed to do something about it.

See, my passion for my entire life has been to cheer on the underdogs. I have always felt like a superhero not because of an over-inflated ego but because when the odds are stacked against someone—which is the case in entrepreneurship and more so for women—it's nice to know that somewhere out there, someone has your back. And ever since I was a little girl, I have felt like that was my job.

But my character has another side. I hate the idea of always having to save people when I know there's a way to change the system to keep people from needing saving in the first place. So, I study. I stay curious. And I stay rebellious. If you tell me something and my gut tells me differently, I figure out who's right and why. And then I tell the world. So, I guess I'm not as much a superhero as I am a vigilante.

That's why I will warn you that sometimes this book is going to feel like I'm talking you out of doing your own thing. But the truth is, I feel like if you are going to jump into entrepreneurship, I want you to do it bigger and better than you ever imagined.

But also living for the first time in my adult life without a spouse or partner for several years, I know how important financial autonomy is for everyone, but more importantly, for women. And since few things we need to survive in this world are free, businesses or careers can be vehicles to take us to lives better than we ever thought possible for ourselves and our families.

So, I thought about if you asked me, *What should I know?* Well, this book is what I wish someone would have told me before I started and failed and started and failed again at my own companies. Because I had talent. Good research. Great people management skills. I was a fucking closer when it came to sales. Long-term visioning and planning. Cash flow projections and budget management. Strategy—all of it. All. Of. It.

But in the end, I didn't know myself nearly as well as I knew my target markets, my customers, or my employees.

So, yes, there are lots of business books written by women who have had some challenges in life but fast-tracked themselves to success. I am not that author, and this is not that book. Instead, this book is built from the rubble of failures.

And I think that's a good thing because the reality is most people are going to fail many, many times. And when they read books by people who made it look easy—almost too easy—and they still can't pull off their own success, it reinforces this sense of inner shame that they are not good enough. And I just can't stand for that. It's not fair when I know the truth and I know how to help them.

That's why I wrote this as a conscious-shifting, life-altering, pulling-back-the-curtains-and-seeing-the-real-wizard, "holy shit" kind of business book. The business book you read *before* you start a business.

So, here's a question then you might ask yourself: how do you know that what I'm writing about works, given the fact that I just told you how often I've messed up? Well, aside from my modest achievements in life, the proof is in the simple fact that you are reading this book.

See, I am living right now in the most challenging era of life I've ever been in—a single mom with two teenagers, overcoming the impacts of abusive relationships, working a full-time job, and pulling myself up and out of financial deficits I created over the years.

Unlike other self-help or business authors, I didn't have an encouraging partner to share the burdens life brought, such as helping with paying the bills, cooking meals, or attending school meetings, so that I would have free time to write this book. Nor was there someone here to offer me a sweet, soft kiss on the forehead at a moment when I may have needed my spirit lifted or my back rubbed. Not to mention, during my writing schedule, the coronavirus swept across the planet, adding a whole other surreal dynamic to everyone's lives that just made things weird and scary. And if I had chosen to give up or slow down, I don't think anyone would have blamed me.

And yet, because of everything I learned and unlearned about myself, I am taking actions to change the course of my future. I am stealing time when I can get it to keep growing myself and to help others along the way. But most importantly, I know how to set a vision for myself so powerful that nothing—not even the worst, loneliest days—can take that mental image away from me and make me quit on it.

I am unstoppable.

Now, lots of people have exactly the life I want—financial security, fulfilling work that changes people's lives, and freedom to travel to every corner of this planet. And there are lots of people that have the life *you* dream about too. You want to know the difference between us and them? It will be here, in these pages.

It is a mastery of ourselves and our minds. It is raising our emotional intelligence. It is debunking myths we've been told about what our roles as women are supposed to be. And it is understanding that the keys to motivation, resilience, money management, assertiveness, planning, and balance are all based on how our human brain processes memories and emotions. Seriously.

So, I want to help you lift the blindfold from your eyes and show you the real world. I want to dismantle your doubts and bad habits and help you rebuild into the woman you need to be to do this. Why?

Because I believe women in business will be a powerful shift in this world and not everything we've been taught is detrimental to us. Our skills and abilities we were groomed to have and which can hold us back also have upsides that make us a different kind of leader in businesses and communities. These skills are needed in this day and age. And the women who recognize that they have this power and awareness in them? Think of the possibilities.

You do not have to want to be a CEO of a huge corporation to benefit from this book. Every single little thing we all do to share our gifts and talents with the world and are rewarded for doing so breathes fresh air into our Universe.

Every woman who gets to fulfill her dreams enriches humanity. When we manifest the lives we were meant to live—not the life someone told us to live—it immediately generates happiness in ourselves that we end up sharing with everyone we come into contact with. It is really that simple.

So, you asked me, "What does it really take to start a business?"

Well, order another round and sit back because, sister, I'm about to tell you.

• • •

Chapter One

PRINCESSES, UNICORNS & ASTRONAUTS

"No matter where you're from, your dreams are valid."

—*Lupita Nyong'o*

What did you want to be when you grew up?

I know that starting with remembering all of the wonder and awe about the world we had as children does not seem like it can have any benefit for deciding what kind of business you want to begin. If you ask any of us what we wanted to be when we grew up, you'd get a myriad of answers that range from ridiculous to insightful, such as a princess, veterinarian, astronaut, rock star, or president of the United States of America.

But there are some truths that can be found in our childhoods that can help us understand who we really are as people. In fact, it's in the purity of childhood—before expectations and grooming fully took over our direction and sense of self—that can help us see who we were always meant to be. And maybe what you wanted to do when you were eight years old is unrealistic, but think about when you were twelve, sixteen, or eighteen years old. I bet you didn't believe in unicorns then, but you did believe in something, right?

My earliest memories of what I wanted to do were to be a writer at five years old.

And I carried my love for writing with me throughout my childhood and into adulthood. I would write poems and send them to the newspaper to be published or writing contests. And when I was in middle school, my entrepreneurial side began to emerge when I began writing poems for classmates and selling them for five dollars each. But most importantly, I was a prolific journal keeper from the age of eleven until I started high school. Writing was, for me, a way to make sense of my inner world.

Having moved around a lot as a child, I did not stay in a single school much longer than one year at a time. But after being at one school for two years, I was identified as "gifted" and given an opportunity to work with a counselor on activities to stimulate my talents and interests, and naturally, I chose writing. So throughout middle school and in high school, I would meet up with the local poet-in-residence in my hometown to hone my skills. And sometimes, for fun, I'd work with musicians so that I could write songs because I also dreamed of being a rock star. In fact, music is my love language.

Unfortunately, I suffered from nightmares growing up, due to post-traumatic stress that wouldn't be diagnosed until my forties. As a result, I developed a passion for the brain and the study of psychology. That's when I began to also use the extracurricular time I was given in high school for studying Freud, Jung, and theorists of psychology and dream analysis.

In fact, back in 1989, at the same time that a new field called "computational neuroscience" was emerging, I wondered if the signals in the brain that allow us to see our own dreams in our minds were similar to the ways the eyes see and deliver information to the brain. So, I theorized that if we could take that signal and put it on a monitor, a psychiatrist could see the dream and its details in order to help a patient neutralize nightmares and make sense of their subconscious. I hadn't quite worked the specifics out, but it seemed like a cool idea!

Now, imagine being a seventeen-year-old girl describing all these ideas to her parent who barely made it out of high school. It sounded more like science fiction and not an actual career. But, while my ideas fell on deaf ears at home, my gifted counselor encouraged me because to her, it seemed I had a clear path and direction to take once I graduated from high school. Looking back, I would agree—it was obvious. But the problem was that, at the time, my family didn't think so.

Instead, I had intense pressure to not be a writer, or a psychologist, or be in music—because those people don't make any money and since no one else in the family is good at it, I was told I won't be either. And despite how much time and effort I spent learning and writing poetry, my mother thought modern poets were weird and it was all fodder for her jokes and teasing.

Now, at the time, my high school boyfriend had an older brother in college who was finishing up his engineering degree, so he also wanted to be an engineer and thought we should do it together. My family latched on the idea and so, it was between him, my family, and my deep feelings to not let any of them down, that being an engineer was what I apparently wanted to do too.

I bet my experience is not that unique because this is how most of our lives play out. During a period of time when decisions are made for you—which is the bulk of a typical American childhood—our independent and autonomous identities are largely ignored and parents either think they need to craft you into mini versions of themselves or into a role that fits their needs or wants better.

And oftentimes, our parents simply lack the skills to understand how to see our true nature, potential, and purpose. And through no fault of their own, they didn't know how to encourage us to grow. Instead, many parents relied on the time-test parenting strategy of "knowing what's best for you." So, even though I had a supportive adult in the form of my gifted counselor—Anne was her name, by the way—it could not overpower the will and influence of my family, so I got an engineering degree just like they wanted.

How does this happen? Why did parenting and childhood look like this for so many people?

First, I have some shocking news: it's because all our families are a little messed up.

Yes, it is true, there is no such thing as the perfect family. Despite a parent's best, most loving intentions, hardships and stressors are a part of life. And there are many stresses in our families these days that are so common, they feel like a normal part of growing up and nothing to be concerned about. Or, more commonly, some of us feel that we've "overcome" them without understanding the real long-term impacts. But just how many of us had to grow up with these hardships and challenging families?

In 1998, a groundbreaking study by the Centers for Disease Control and Kaiser Permanente showed the relationship of adverse childhood experiences, known as ACES, we have in our first eighteen years of life to adult health problems. Aside from seeing how adversities and trauma in childhood increase the risk for developing health conditions, the other major findings were that these ACES occur **across all socioeconomic, racial, and gender populations and that roughly two-thirds of all households have at least one ACE**. Additionally, about 20 percent of adults in the study experienced three or more ACES in the first eighteen years of life. And, in the results of the study, more women reported three or more ACES in their lives than men!

So, what are these ACES? Well, they include witnessing or experiencing emotional or physical abuse, including spanking and yelling. ACES also include living in poverty, having a parent with substance problems like alcoholism, sexual abuse, emotional neglect, and even divorce. In fact, further research has shown that other experiences can be traumatic or stressful for children and have long-term impacts on our health like experiencing racism, being bullied or teased, watching a sibling being abused, surviving the death of a parent or other close family member, and so forth.

While some of the experiences seem like obvious traumas, I've met and spoken with a lot of people and many never think about, for example, being spanked as a child or having a parent yell in your face when they were angry because everyone's parents did that. And so, a lot of people don't view their childhoods as "adverse" but only normal. Finally, most of us look at the list and can, for example, identify with growing up with divorced parents and think that it's also no big deal because that is your past and has nothing to do with you today. And yet the evidence says otherwise for many of us.

WHO WE ARE:
NATURE VS. NURTURE?

We all know the age-old question, "Is it nature or is it nurture?" that makes us who we are. And thanks to advances in science and research, we now know the answer is that it's a bit of both. And that's why I'm challenging you, as you read this next section, to question how much of who you believe you are and what you believe you want is related to how you learned to fit into your family or is an authentic expression of who you really are.

Now, when families have some degree of dysfunction, even if it's a temporary situation like a divorce, human brains work to manage or fix this dysfunction within our family system. And one way is to create order through family members settling into **roles**.

I know I don't need to tell you that family dynamics are complicated, even in "good" families. And most of us, at one point or another, end up falling into a position or role within our families. Roles in families end up bringing order to dynamics, but especially if the home and family we grew up in was disorganized or under stress. Sometimes the parent's assign roles to their children and sometimes children develop them on their own. But the problem is that a role we played in our family was a survival tactic and may not actually be reflective of our true selves.

This concept of seeing these roles develop in families in place of authentic identities was first presented by family therapist and author Virginia Satir in 1988. By studying families for decades, she noted that the role a child assumes in the family is in response to compensating for dysfunctions in communication. She also saw that this role becomes the basis for shaping the personality of the adult the child grows into. But sadly, she noted that the roles a child played easily overwhelmed an individual's ability to be themselves. In other words, the better you played your part, the harder it became to change.

Over the years, researchers and therapists have seen five major roles develop in families, and while they may have slightly different names, my favorite breakdown is here:

- **The Hero**, often the oldest sibling who is responsible for solving the family's problems.

- **The Golden Child**, lives on a pedestal of achievements and is the center of attention.
- **The Scapegoat**, always in trouble, blamed for problems, or refuses to follow the family rules.
- **The Mascot**, often the youngest, who uses humor to shift focus from discomfort or dysfunction.
- **The Lost Child**, the one who feels like the outsider in their own family and disappears.

If you begin to reflect on your family today and as a child, do you notice if you had or currently have a role? Sometimes we know what role we played by any nicknames people in your family gave you. Were you the "Smart One" or the "Jock" or the "Clown?" Were you "Mother's Little Helper" or "Daddy's Girl?" Were you the "Big Sister" or the "Baby" in the family?

As you grew older, did your role change a bit, say from the Golden Child to the Scapegoat when you got into high school? Or was your role less obvious, but you were always told things like, "Oh honey, I don't know what we'd ever do without you." Or did you become the one your mother asked for advice all the time or your father complained to?

Often, we started playing a role in our family to gain our parents' attention, but how important it was for us stay in that role to make the family dynamics livable for everyone depended on our family of origin's levels of dysfunction and **differentiation.**

While we do have inherited qualities in us that define our temperament, it is also true that our family system influences our sense of "self." Dr. Murray Bowen, a psychiatrist, originated a theory of human behavior that a family was one interconnected, emotional unit. This means that families tend to groupthink and the emotions of everyone in the family feed off one another. People in the family will vary in how susceptible they are to this, due to nature and nurture, and this variability impacts a person's ability to develop a high or low sense of self-identity.

People with a low sense or poorly differentiated sense of self rely on acceptance and approval from other people. It's as if how well they are doing in life can only be determined by what others think of them or do for them. On one side of the low-self coin, a person may always be adjusting themselves to fit or appease another person's view of them. While on the other side of the coin, a person may be manipulating the people around them to get everyone to conform to their standards.

So, for example, if you have a parent or caregiver who has a low sense of self, their viewpoint is that you are an extension of themselves. Your emotions are their emotions. And if you are upset, they want you to stop being upset so that they can stop being upset. If you want to do something that they would never do, they work to interfere with that or prohibit you because it doesn't fit their own needs, or it raises discomfort for them.

To manage their discomfort, a parent might control how you dress or what music you could listen to, as well as what activities you are forced to do or not allowed to do, like music or sports. This type of parental control tactics can range from the passive-aggressive use of guilt to punishments for not doing what they want you to do. They are attempting to create you in their image because it's easier for them to handle or because they think they can.

See, throughout most of history, a guiding thought was that all children are born as a **blank slate** and are the property of their parents, so we could be made into anything they wanted us to be. This theory can be traced back to Aristotle but was made very well known by seventeenth century empiricist John Locke. Simply put, the belief latched onto by parents and educators was that all of us are born needing to have our caregivers tell us what to do, how to think, and how to behave.

So this idea of a blank slate set a tone in parenting and our educational systems that made it seem like you could write onto any child's mind who you wanted them to be through repetition, punishment, fear, and consequences. If there was resistance to the desired outcomes, nobody knew that it was just the child's true individual nature rebelling. Instead, it must mean that the tactics were wrong and perhaps greater force needed to be applied.

The result was that as your own natural personality started to emerge, if your parents didn't notice or nurture it, but instead they pressured you to change, you didn't actually change who you really were and you learned to simply adapt. And today, this all is considered emotional neglect—the disregard and dismissiveness of a child's temperament and emotional needs, which is also an ACE.

If, however, you had parents or caregivers with a high or well-differentiated sense of self, they could easily see that everyone is an individual and that your emotions, behaviors, and needs were your own and they didn't feel a need to sequester or control them. It doesn't mean that your choices don't impact them emotionally, but it does mean that they are not at the mercy of those feelings. They were likely calmer and didn't feel threatened as you began to individuate. You were likely given room to explore and flourish. And to be honest, if this was your entire family, you are probably in the minority.

In the end, when we have a family dynamic with a lot of people with poorly differentiated self-identities, it means we may have grown up with the overarching specter of needing to gain approval or acceptance from others. And this may have included completely giving up on what we want or believe just to make someone else happy.

Dr. Lindsay Gibson, the author of *Recovering from Emotionally Immature Parents*, points out that parents with low self-differentiation tend to be quick to judge and ridicule other people's inner worlds or "inner self." In extreme cases, some of us grow up with a fear of expressing who we really are and what we really believe in. The constant barrage of questioning and dismissiveness directed toward us about what we want or feel then creates a lack of trust with our own inner world and cuts us off from our own awareness of our life's purpose.

The emotionally immature parent then may invalidate your dreams and undercut your decisions because you threaten their existence. They can't see you as anything other than extension of themselves or the overall family identity. So, to survive this environment and to maintain our connection with our parents (or risk the loss of their love and acceptance), we turn against our own thoughts and we learn to build a façade. We shut down and play the role in the family drama to make life easier for ourselves and not rock the boat.

But let me point out something important here too; our parents or caregivers probably loved us, cared about us, and just wanted what they thought was best for us. In fact, that is probably truly the case for many of you reading this. And as children, we are wired to maintain our connection with our caregivers because it's a matter of life or death—we need them to want us and take care of us.

So, when well-meaning adults are telling us what they want us to do or want us to be, even if inside of us it doesn't feel quite right, we are apt to follow their guidance just because, at the end of the day, we don't want to break that connection. Children are, by nature, people-pleasing. That means being sidelined from pursuing your dreams or not doing something you're talented in and passionate about is oftentimes the tragic result of the interactions between loving human beings who simply didn't know the long-term consequences of what they were doing to one another.

And the wonderful thing about life is that while you may have put your own pursuits on hold in order to be what your parents and caregivers wanted for you many years ago, you don't have to keep doing it anymore if you don't want to.

THE FAMILY BELIEF SYSTEM

Beliefs that our families held can be like fingerprints smudging up the screen on a smart phone. They can distort our views, even slightly, and despite our attempts to wipe them away, they seem to come back again. And we will keep coming back to them in this book because they can have a huge impact on our success as entrepreneurs in many areas when we don't realize we're unconsciously following them.

And what's tricky is that beliefs are not just the words we heard our families say, but they are also communicated through the actions and behaviors we witnessed. And furthermore, what can be really messed up is that we humans tend to say one thing but model something different, hence the saying we all know so well: actions speak louder than words. In other words, we might have been getting mixed messages.

And so, beliefs about the world we learned from our family can be really sneaky and tough to tease out. Our family may have told us that having a good paying job was important but at the same time, referred to wealthy people as corrupt. Or they may have been proud of you for being an exemplary math student, but, at the same time, the women in your family said that money and finances were the man's job.

Some family beliefs relate to the family identity and may sound like "We're working-class people" or "We aren't musical people" or "We are football people." They could also be expectations set for everyone that live or work in the same town, family business, or the same career fields. These kinds of beliefs could be putting pressure on you to not reject them for fear of losing your place in your family, leaving you feeling guilty or ashamed for wanting to choose something different for yourself. And this guilt could be internal resistance for you that keeps you from pursuing your true passions.

You may have seen and decided for yourself that you didn't believe in some beliefs such as racism, sexism, or hate. And you have adopted some beliefs without realizing it because they were communicated through actions and behaviors modeled for you as a child, and you ended up copying them.

Now, some beliefs are worth holding onto if they are healthy for you. And by that, a positive belief is something that is built on integrity and does not rely on one person or groups of people's rights or needs to be diminished in favor of another person's wants. Beliefs that are fair, just, and balanced are not only worth keeping, but worth fighting for.

That does not mean, however, a belief that relies on you putting yourself last to everyone else around you all the time is positive, even if you've been groomed to think that. For example, always setting aside your needs or even wants because you have a "responsibility" to take care of other people first sounds noble but isn't fair to *you*.

Likewise, a belief that seems harmless but hurts a lot of women is that we are supposed to hand over major financial responsibilities and decisions in a relationship to the other person and let them "handle it." Unfortunately, the evidence shows that this sets you up to be vulnerable if that other person leaves you or dies or chooses to manipulate and control you. Again, this is something we're definitely going to keep talking about.

One viewpoint that always teeters on the edge of good and bad is "Keep trying harder." On one hand, it inspires you to work through difficulties and not give up when things get hard. But on the other hand, it can also keep you trapped in situations that are unwinnable.

Also, through this groupthink environment with our family, we pick up on their worldviews, and even if through our own maturation and growth we change our opinions or ideas about something, we still carry the influence of the original thoughts inside of us. And, unfortunately, this influence rears its ugly heads in the form of inner voices of self-doubt or unconscious beliefs about ourselves.

QUITTING THE PLAY

Some people may feel that in their family, they had a pretty clear part in the family drama. However, most of us throughout our lives have played different roles at different times. Or we played more than one at the same time. In this case, the weight of these roles feels like wearing a bunch of sweaters at the same time, all layered on themselves, limiting movements and feeling terribly uncomfortable.

Roles are so familiar to us because they were the norm for a significant part of our lives. You may not have ever known, however, that you were playing a role, let alone which one. So how can you tell? Well, you will know you are playing a role when you visit with your family and you slide into old patterns, behaviors, or habits that you do not usually do when you are living independently.

I noticed that when I went home to visit family that my usually light-hearted and laid-back demeanor shifted substantially. I would become tense, uptight, and ready for confrontation. Growing up as a teenager and even young adult, I used to say that I could not take a joke. But I am actually a pretty funny person. What I discovered, after some time, was that at my family's home, teasing and making fun of me was a role I filled for some of them. I was taunted for my beliefs they didn't share or for my interests in subjects that they didn't understand. So, of course I couldn't take a joke—I was a child who grew up being the butt of the jokes!

But I was also the Hero Child—the Problem Solver. As I became older, my role shifted to that of the Scapegoat—the Truth Teller. I began to rebel and stand up for my own needs and principles. But when none of that seemed to matter or change the people around me, I finally became the Lost Child and moved away for good at eighteen years old. The burden of being all these things was overwhelming for most of my life. In fact, even after moving away, I unconsciously replayed these roles in other settings, like my own family and in my businesses. But once I learned what was going on, I finally decided in my forties to throw my script down and walk off the stage.

See, playing one or many roles in our families for years distorts our views of ourselves in the world with others. Some of us get stuck being in this role outside of the family that cast us in the part. We think we need to be the hero all the time, for example. And maybe we do. Sometimes the skills we learned in these roles are truly the best things about us. But the difference is that you learn to know when you *want* to be that person versus when you feel you *need* to be that person. Are you rising to the occasion out of a sense of purpose or someone else's expectations?

So how do you quit the part in the family drama so that you can begin to become your truer self? Well, you have to start with getting honest with yourself and ask yourself these three questions.

WHAT BENEFITS AM I GETTING WHEN I PLAY MY ROLE?

Yes, there can be benefits for you in playing an old role, even a role that seems to come with bad side-effects. For example, you might say you are tired from having to point out the family's problems, but when you are able to make a solid point, don't you get a feeling of satisfaction from being right?

Or maybe as the hero, you are exhausted from having to be the one in the family who takes care of everyone and solves the family's problems, so why do you keep doing it?

Is that because you get to tell yourself what a good person you are for sacrificing your needs for others? Is it because of the gratitude others show you for helping them? You know, it's okay to admit that you like being thanked for being helpful. That's not always a terrible benefit unless it comes at the cost of your own needs.

But sometimes, playing our role feels like the path of least resistance too. That is, it's easier to just continue to go along with everything than it is to deal with the discomfort of changing, which is also a perceived benefit to you. But ask yourself: whose discomfort are you avoiding? Yours or someone else's? Is avoiding someone else's anger or sadness because you've chosen to break ranks feel easier to deal with than making the change?

If that's the case, then here's something I want you to consider: why do you think your anger or sadness at doing something you despise is less important than someone else's? Because you're tougher or stronger than the other person and you can handle it (a beneficial lie you keep telling yourself)? Or is it really because you have never simply considered or been shown that your feelings and needs matter too?

Whether we realize it or not, we are getting a reward in some form from staying in our roles, even if that reward is just the lesser of two evils. So, be honest with yourself here with this one because this question can be the most revealing. Do you play your role because you can avoid negative emotions from other people? Or do you play the role because when you do, people pat you on the back and it makes you feel "wanted" even if you had to give up your own needs to do it?

WHAT ARE THE BENEFITS I WILL GET WHEN I STOP PLAYING MY ROLE?

Now, let's flip the script and consider a wild idea: what if you stopped playing your role today? What benefits would you get then? So, in our hypothetical world, where no one knows that right now you are thinking of quitting the family drama, think about the rewards that await you for breaking free.

For example, would you be able to spend time doing something you have always wanted to do instead of spending time helping everyone else out? Would you have more money for yourself instead of giving it away to help other people every time they ask you? Would you just have more mental resources because you are not worrying about the next shoe to drop with your parents or siblings? Would your anxiety levels decrease? Would your happiness increase if you simply no longer gave a shit about other people's opinions of what you should or shouldn't be doing? Of course, it would! Happy people do amazing things!

WHO WOULD I BECOME IF I DIDN'T PLAY MY ROLE ANYMORE?

I had a coaching session once with a woman who had grown up in her family of origin in the hero role. She came to me with a podcast idea based on her experiences of figuring out how to care for her aging parents and to share this advice with other Gen-X's who have Boomer parents. She showed up to the session ready to jump into the "hows" and wanted me to coach her on how to start.

When she introduced herself to me, she said she was a listener of my show and we talked a little about her parents. She easily identified them as the emotionally immature types who, along with a younger sister, all relied on her to pick up their slack her entire life. In other words, she was the hero in her family. And while I felt that she had a great idea in the works with a real need in the world, as I listened to her story, I heard several things that made me wonder about what was truly driving her to pursue this.

I kept quiet as she laid out a rough form of what she was thinking and what she should do next, and then I leaned back in my chair and asked, "Where do you see yourself in five years?" She paused.

"Well, I'm not sure. I mean guess if I start with a website..." I stopped her.

"No, I'm not talking about this business idea. Where do **you** want to be in five years?"

After a few long moments, she replied, "I really don't know. I hadn't thought about it."

I could hear in her story that she had spent so much time and energy living and "begrudgingly" playing her part that she had not given any thought to what her life could be like not playing the role of her family's rescuer.

I asked if her parents were financially set and had caregivers taking care of them now and she said, "Yes."

I continued, "So, you accomplished your mission, and you have nothing left to do for them. You are not needed here anymore, right?"

And she replied, "Yeah, I guess you're right."

I then went on and said, "I think you need to take some time to think about the answer to my question because I'm concerned that you are trading the enslavement of being your parents' keeper for another form of it. You seem to still want to carry the torch from taking care of them even though you just said you don't need to anymore. So, make sure that what you are thinking of doing is going to put you where you really want to be. Because your parents aren't always going to be here, and you can now start to figure out who you really are without them. You're still young and have potentially another forty years to live."

She stared back at me and then leaned back in her chair. I could see the lights coming on inside her head and she was beginning to see the exit doors.

I told her that before worrying about whether she should do a website or start a podcast or write a book, that she would first have to detox from her role, allowing the feelings of "needing" to do things to come and go. And, having been a hero myself, I told her it wasn't going to happen overnight, but it would be the most important thing she'd do for herself and bring her the best clarity around what her next steps really should be.

Sadly, her story and situation are not unique. Our strongest compulsions to "do something" can be pure expressions of our true selves and purpose or they can be the powerful forces from our childhood roles that we don't know how to quit playing. But they are not the same and it really is important to understand the difference. Now, while I could have been willing to continue to help her develop a strategy for her idea, I believe in results and happiness. And building out a launch plan for a person who doesn't have a destination chosen just feels like putting them in a rocket and blasting them out into space and leaving them to float. That just seems cruel.

So, what happened with her? Several months later, she did start a podcast after all—about her passion for traveling.

Now all this might make sense to you right up until the minute you have to let go of the edge and break free. And then it gets scary. And that's because humans are like many creatures on this planet in that we run in herds or packs. There is safety in numbers, and over the course of two million years, we've seen evidence of the human species gathering in tribes, clans, and gated communities.

That why is when you want to change, your herd of friends or family can become threatened and pressure you to not do it. Or you can feel a sense of primal fear from deciding to go along a different way because it can leave you feeling alone and exposed to the dangers of the world. In any case, change is hard. And so, deciding to break free from roles and beliefs that you don't want to play will come with resistance—outside and inside.

The desire to maintain cohesion within our communities follows us out of our family of origin and into other circles we join in life such as work, volunteer groups, networking and professional groups, and even our friendships.

On top of this, women have historically been put into positions throughout their childhood and adult lives in which we are responsible for maintaining connection and cohesiveness, often at the expense of our opinions or needs. So, when a woman is placed in a situation that asks her to break connection, either with family or friends or peers, due to this grooming, it feels, well, even more weird. And to make matters worse, other women can view it as threatening to themselves, especially if they have lower levels of self-differentiation and self-awareness.

So, depending on the level of dysfunction, cut-offs might be necessary in order to reboot the family or friend system. As I mentioned before, we have nervous systems that interact with each other, so it might also be important to give yourself some physical and emotional space during this time.

Some people worry that this act of rebellion against the herd is permanent, but it doesn't have to be. Whether or not it is will depend highly on yourself as well as your herd, but it is possible to reestablish connection again once you have been able to shed a few of the sweater layers you don't want to wear anymore.

But let's say you don't need a full cut-off from your family or friends. What if, for example, you just stopped telling your mom your opinions on how she should handle her problems with your brother when she called? Or what if you stopped being the person who coordinated all of the family gatherings? What would you do with the extra time and mental energy? What if you just started to tell someone in your family that a joke at your expense was not funny and you are not going to allow it anymore, and then you actually hold your boundary when it happens again—how would that make you feel?

What I'm saying is that this isn't easy. And if you decide bucking the system is going a little too far for you, that's your choice and you wouldn't be alone in that. But before you skip the rest of this book, I'm going to ask you to consider the last question of this section: if the opinions of your parents, friends, or family didn't matter, what would you be doing instead? And is that worth giving up?

And we are going to keep talking about this many times in the book because the people you choose to have in your life are an invaluable part of your success as an entrepreneur and in life.

WHO YOU REALLY ARE

As we are winding down here in this chapter, we are now ready to pull out a blank page and do an inventory.

To do this, put away the specifics of the business idea or concept that you are thinking about and that prompted you to buy a book about starting a business. Let us dial things back a bit. Now that I've shown the light in a few corners of your attic of memories and experiences, I want you to take an inventory of yourself, regardless of profession or personal environment. I want you to begin to see who you really are.

I know I started this chapter with asking you to remember what you wanted to be when you were a kid, but, truthfully, coming back to that question can be a little misleading because in all honesty, vocations and jobs are interchangeable. So, what if you wanted to be a veterinarian growing up and didn't? I'm not telling you that if you changed your path and got that job, you'd be happy.

What I'm saying is that we have parts of us that are true and pure to who we really are that are beyond our jobs or what we have on our résumés. And what's important is that sometimes our vocations and the briefcases we carry around guide us toward entrepreneurship because the years of experience we have in one industry or another must mean that we should be our own bosses, right?

For example, if you got an accounting degree years ago because your family thought it would be a good choice for you and you've made it work all these years, it doesn't necessarily mean that starting your own accounting firm will be more fulfilling. Nor do your years of experience as an accountant solely guarantee your business venture will be successful. That is, unless you really do have a passion for it.

So right now, get your blank page ready and strip away as much as you can of expectations, pressures, and opinions that didn't feel "right." Let's figure out who you really are.

EXERCISE

1. What did you want to do when you grew up? List out all the things you thought at one time or another you'd be doing once you became an adult.
2. List out all of the things you have been passionate about in your life, like causes, hobbies, or lifestyles.
3. List out your key talents and abilities that come naturally to you and make you unique.

I'm sure you wrote out a lot of really great skills and talents that you know you have. But what if you still don't know what to make of them? It's quite possible that what you are good at is not so much a particular talent or skill but could be your commitment and belief in your feeling of purpose or direction. And the reason you want to start your own business is that you are trying to find the outlet to express it.

Many of us may be good at a variety of skills—maybe too good—and can easily move from job to job or even different industries altogether. If you are not one of these people, you certainly have seen them—they are always on the search for the next big thing. So, confusing our talents and skills for what it is we are "meant" to do can be problematic.

Anna, a West Point grad turned army helicopter pilot turned corporate engineer turned wedding photographer, found herself realizing this after years of trying on different careers. That is when she shifted her thinking from the job she wanted to do to what *life* she wanted to live. "As cheesy at it sounds, I have always wanted to change the world. And I felt like I lived many lives and tried many things, but no matter what I did, I wasn't fulfilled."

So, if you think that maybe you could be in Anna's shoes now in your life and that's why you are pursuing entrepreneurship, you could really benefit from this next exercise.

EXERCISE

1. After looking at childhood, what do you feel is your most authentic worldview and role in life? What do you think you were meant to do? Are you doing that today? Why?
2. After looking at your passions & interests, which ones stand out as having the most meaning and inspiration? Do you do any of them now? Why?
3. After considering your talents & skills, which do you feel are the most useful and purposeful? Are you practicing or using any of them now? Why?
4. Are these in alignment with the business you were thinking of starting? If not, what's different?

REMEMBERING YOUR PURPOSE

Since the ACES study was published, there have been over seventy follow-up studies confirming the results and changing the way people view parenting, childhood development, mental health, and chronic illnesses. It also confirmed that most of us have experienced during our first eighteen years of life some adversity or challenge that affected us or our parents or both. And nearly half of us have grown up with several chronic family challenges which altered our lives more deeply than science ever realized. And these challenges stem mostly from the internal workings of our families such as how they view life, how they view themselves, and how these views get passed down from generation to generation.

These challenges, combined with errant childhood development theories that have since been proven wrong, have left most of us with some misguided sense of what life is supposed to be like. And at some deep level, many of us feel the disconnect between what we want and what someone has told us we should want.

We also know that while growing up, we were a part of a dynamic and complex family system. Understanding this can help us make sense of how we continue to live as adults. We will continue to explore this beyond this chapter because it's vital to your success in life and as a businessperson, to know how the software in your head was programmed.

So, if you have this amazing set of skills, passions, and interests but are not using them in any way today, it could mean that you are stuck playing out a role or expectation someone else or the dynamics of your family of origin ingrained in you. And we can begin to un-stick you.

But what if you don't like your answers? What if it feels like life is too complex today for you to simply read one chapter in one book and have it all suddenly figured out? Does that mean you can't continue with the idea of starting your own business? That you failed at step one?

No. That's not it at all. You do not have to know it all today. In fact, you might very well still be on the path of trying new things and sorting out what you love and care about, and that is okay too! And to be honest, those things that energize us do change over time and through our circumstances. One minute, you're a single woman, fresh out of college and what excites you is the idea of traveling the world with a grunge band as their photographer, and then the next thing you know, you're a mom and what excites you is cleaning up the planet so that your children have a world worth living in. I was that woman. Both are pure and honest feelings inspired by the times I was living in.

And so, I hope that you are beginning to understand why I dragged you through your family history and an introduction to psychology. It's because before we can talk about **how** to start a business, we must know **why** you want to start a business. And before we know why you want to do that, we must know if it's really **your goal** and ambition or someone else's. Because if you are still on a path of living out the life someone else wanted for you, you will feel it in your bones. It won't succeed simply because it won't be authentic.

Guaranteed. Whereas if you are finally pursuing your deepest dreams and aspirations, nothing is going to stop you.

Now, despite how it reads, this chapter isn't a manifesto on parenting gone wrong and how we are all victims of our childhood. But if this is the only chapter you read in this book, I simply want you to be able to sit with this information. See if you can't reframe your life in a way that helps you really figure out how everything along your own timeline has come together. There is a happy ending.

In a conversation I had with Lindsay Gibson, she shared with me the story from Greek mythology about the Goddess of Necessity. Before a soul enters the earth, they must sit on the Goddess's lap and she whispers into their ear what their purpose will be in the life to come. And as soon as she whispers it into their ear, the Goddess presses her finger onto the mouth, leaving the little indention we all have above our lips. Once that happens, the soul forgets what was whispered and then goes into the earth and the soul spends the rest of their life trying to remember what the Goddess told them.

When I heard that story, I teared up. Because I remembered a beautiful moment in late 2017 when I realized that not pursuing writing and psychology right away was not something my family stole from me, but a gift. I reflected back on the fact that, instead of doing what I wanted, I moved forward with a life that wasn't entirely my own. That helped me understand how that really felt and what happens to us in parenting, relationships, and business when we do that. And then, only after living like this, running into setbacks on my journey, and becoming insanely curious about my experiences, a light came on. And then I knew—like, I really knew—that now was the time to be who I was supposed to be because I had something worth writing about. I remembered what the Goddess had whispered to me.

Those innate passions I always had were not lost. They were there all along, like the foundation of an ancient colosseum buried in the dirt. And they became the base I needed to deconstruct the old and rebuild, not a "new me," but the **real me**. They were waiting until I remembered my Goddess-given purpose. And yours are too.

Chapter Two

WHY ARE YOU DOING THIS?

"Begin with the end in mind."

–Stephen R. Covey

One of the biggest things I learned in my entrepreneurial life was how important a vision for a life you want to live is to business success. I have always had a rich imagination, and so thinking about some awesome future for myself comes pretty naturally. But using it as a guide for choices to make in my business was something I learned after many years of taking routes that directed me *away* from what I really wanted.

Now, it really doesn't take a lot of work to start a business. You don't need a special degree or certification from anyone to decide one day that you want to be self-employed. And running a business once it's started is also not that hard. You know this because running a business is what employees do: turning the lights on, answering the phone and emails, paying the bills—keeping the machine running. If there's a system in place to streamline some of these activities, running a business can almost be on autopilot, which works amazingly when everything is moving along smoothly and predictably.

Where it all falls apart is in *doing* a business. I know this not a phrase that is commonly used, but I like the word because "doing" means taking actions to get something done. By definition, it means there are goals, objectives, planning, and having to keep your eye on a target and doing whatever it takes to hit the target.

So, not understanding the nuances between "running" and "doing" is where business owners fail. If they expect that all things will go smoothly if all the right machines are running, then when something breaks down, they are lost, frustrated, and may quit. However, if an entrepreneur knows that nothing goes according to plan because life is full of uncertainty, then they are undaunted and don't get discouraged when they have to break form and think strategically about what they need to *do* next.

Let me illustrate this further and better.

I love a good road trip. Miles in a car with my head swiveling around, taking in every detail along the way. Pit stops for gross food from a convenience store or jumping out with my camera at a viewpoint and being in awe at what Mother Nature has done. I also love driving through an old, forgotten small town and trying to decipher its history through its buildings.

But there is always a point to my road trip—there is a destination in mind. And at this destination is something I want or want to do. But to get from my home to this destination, I know I have to plan the route I will take and figure out how long I have to journey there and how much money it will cost. And I also plan for adjustments, hazards, or other scenarios that could impact the trip. But I don't change where I am going. I just keep an open mind in case I need to be flexible along the way.

Now, many people talk about a "road map" as a tool for planning, so this is not a unique analogy, but we all know from real life that having a map laid out on your kitchen table is very different from getting in the car and actually driving, isn't it?

It's through my experience with working with small businesses and solopreneurs that when they want to start or even improve a business and reach out to me for help, they are not planning for the long-term. They are essentially "car shopping."

Yes, when people decide that they are going to start a business, what they really end up doing is spending time thinking about the car they want to drive, not a destination they want to drive *to*.

They look at what other people are driving, they do some research on features, and when they find one that fits the budget and has what they need, they buy it. And then they turn the key, fire up the engine, and now they have started their business. They put the car into drive, pull out of the driveway, and go. And now they are running their business.

They measure the "success" of the business based on whether the car looks like everyone else's or if other people "like" their car. Don't believe me? Look at social media.

But where are they going? Where is this car taking them? In what direction are they heading? Are they planning on driving until it runs out of gas? Or is the plan to do endless laps around the block until the end of the day, then park the car in the driveway, go inside the house, and begin again in the morning? Where do they see themselves in five or even ten years? Remember the woman from the last chapter I told you about, all gung-ho with the "how" but not a clue on the "where?"

If you are right where you want to be, and you love to drive and don't care where you are going, well, you don't need your own business for that. You can work for any company and drive their car all day long. But sometimes a person gets sick of sitting in the seat of someone else's car, and they think that being in business for themselves will be different. And maybe it will be.

So, they go out, buy their own car, and then drive *it* around the block endlessly. At first it feels good to be in their own car, but then it gets boring and they might feel like they still aren't getting the satisfaction they hoped for. Once they also realize that not only are they just as bored with going nowhere, but now they must pay for their own gas, insurance, and maintenance on this car, they quit self-employment. They become just another start-up business failure statistic.

Here's the secret to succeeding in entrepreneurship: It's not about the car. It's about the destination. In fact, you can start with whatever car you have right now. You can trade it in as you go along the way. Or you can invest in the best car money can buy from day one, but without a destination, it won't take you anywhere.

So, when it comes to planning a vacation, how do you pick your destination? Is it random? Probably not. There is possibly some nostalgia mixed in with adventure. There could be comfort. It could be that you are wanting to go someplace where you feel the most you. We tend to choose our vacations as places to escape from work and stress and participate in the socially acceptable habit of finding work-life balance.

I do know, however, that when I am planning trips, I am not daydreaming about ski trips or spending countless hours out in the cold and snow. I like sun. I like a nice beach, but I also like vistas and wide, broad horizons. I love history and culture and I love to learn new things. I love to do something that makes my heart pump and my adrenaline surge. I love being inspired. I **hate** being cold.

So, as strongly as I know exactly where I'm going, I also know where I'm **not**.

Now, have you ever been on a trip and found out that there is construction work or an accident that cut off a portion of your route or would slow you down if you didn't change course? Did you decide at that time that, instead of continuing to Disneyland since you were now heading east, your destination would change to Phoenix? Of course, you didn't! Your heart is set on Disneyland. The plan is to go to Disneyland. So, who cares if the route needs an adjustment— you adjust and continue, right?

But in entrepreneurship, these hazards or route changes tend to completely derail people because they don't even know where they are going. They just let the GPS plot them a new route, and off they go. They think that driving *is* the reason for the business. And if the car is moving, they are running their business and that feels like they are doing it right. But it's just driving, staying in motion without any thought of where they are going or why they want to go there. And then suddenly, the business they were excited about starting now feels like just another job—because that's what it is.

Ever meet anyone who started a business after years of being an employee and then they quit after a year or two? Did they tell you why? Was it because it turned out that what they loved about their job was doing the work they were an expert in and then discovered self-employment involved doing a lot of other stuff they hated? When a would-be business owner is faced with this fact, they usually make one of two choices— they quit and go back to being an employee or they hire out the work they have a distaste for and run out of money quickly. And then they quit.

I've seen this many times in my career. It's the photographer who hated financials and bookkeeping. The jewelry maker who hated sales and marketing. Even the baker who, believe it or not, actually hated all the time she had to spend baking to fill big orders!

The truth is that you likely won't love everything about doing your business. But that isn't going to stop you because you realize that you have to take the good with the bad in order to get where you're going. You'll take the setbacks with the successes. The construction zones with the long, straight highways and no speed limits because at the end is Disneyland. Or Tahiti. Or more time with your family. Or wherever it is you really want to go.

That brings us to the big point I am trying to make here: in order to stay committed to doing your business, you need to have a reason for why you are taking on this challenge that means something to you. The people who succeed at fulfilling their dreams have in them this powerful energy that inflates their chest and their heart every day—even on bad days—that says, "I'm doing this because I can see my future ahead and I want it badly!"

The big secret is that being an entrepreneur is not driving a car around the block—that's what employees do. It's about seeing a place you want to be out there on the horizon and *going there*. So, let's lay the map out on the table and start to get you thinking about out where you are going.

THINKING LIKE A MOGUL

After all this analogy about cars, vacations, and destinations, am I saying that the vehicle doesn't matter? No, of course it matters. If your destination, metaphorically or literally, involves crossing an ocean, you are not going to be able to *drive* there. And if your goals are to reach your new life and lifestyle in five years, but you have to start it on foot, you may not reach it in time if you don't pick up speed along the way. The point I want to make is that too many people think that buying a car is the goal when it really comes down to where you want to go and where you see yourself as a result of driving this car.

So, now that you spent some time listing out your skills, passions, and talents as well as revisiting some long-lost dreams, let's begin to sort out the business you really want to start and why.

To figure this out, let's first throw away any prejudices you may have regarding businesses structures and organizational charts. Let's not worry about what other people are doing or how they are doing it because the truth is, they may not have the same goals and objectives you have or will have. In fact, they may not have goals or objectives at all!

Most people start and operate their business by looking at how someone else is doing it and then simply copying them. And maybe what you ultimately come up with will look similar at some point, but let's get to that some other time.

For now, let's start by again looking at this as a journey. Cast your eyes out to the horizon in the direction you want to go, and visualize yourself out there at your destination.

And now ask yourself, "Why do I want to have my **own** business?"

Really think about this question for a moment, but also think back to when you first had this thought. What was going on in your life at that time? Were you feeling trapped at a desk in an office? Or have you taken some time off from work and want to reenter the workforce again?

Many people become entrepreneurs because they are attracted to the freedom that it can provide (emphasis on the word "can"). So, it is important why you think you have to be self-employed versus just finding another job at a different company.

Also, how many of you are exploring entrepreneurship because you have a hobby you really like and think you could make some money doing it? Now, how many of you want to build a business that allows you to take *command* and control of your future once and for all? Because, ladies, those are vastly different reasons. And one is not better than the other, but mistaking them as being the same can be costly.

Hobbies are typically associated with things like crafts or creative works, whether that is jewelry making, photography, painting, or even writing. In these cases, what you are selling is linked to your personal efforts and output. But you could also view a hobby-business as any endeavor in which all of your revenue is based on you trading one hour of your time or one unit of what you make for a fixed dollar. That means consulting, coaching, and contracting can also fall into this category as well as well.

These types of businesses can make you money, but they can end up being break-even endeavors for most solopreneurs or one-woman operations if not properly designed. And that's due to **scale** or the ability to grow your business as efficiently as possible. In other words, scaling is being able to increase the products of your business, whether it's bracelets or coaching hours, without an increase in the expenses that negate the potential revenues.

This is the part of business where many, many one-woman operations trip themselves up so much so that it forces them to close their businesses completely. I have cautioned several who come to me with the idea of getting ready to "grow" their business by hiring their first employees because they want to increase their output. The problem is they haven't yet understood the very real costs of doing it. Now, trust me, it makes sense when they tell me that they are at a point of turning away work, or they can't fill bigger orders. But they end up making a miscalculated move based on the idea that they just need one more of themselves to make it work, which is hobby owner thinking.

See, you alone simply have a finite number of hours to sell. And if you have a craft, for example, that you insist must be created with your own two hands, you have a finite capacity that you can produce. This means, overall, your inventory is limited because you cannot be duplicated, nor can you wake up one morning and just decide that you can suddenly double your production. Your craft has a fixed set of steps, and these steps have fairly fixed set of time associated with completing them, known as **cycle time** in manufacturing. Sure, as we get better with a craft, our speed improves, but we are humans, after all, and 100 percent efficiency is an illusion and does not exist in nature or technology.

But this is what most hobby owners also miss: while you are doing the work of making or creating your product (including coaching meetings with clients), you have reduced your available time to do the other work that improves the efficiency of your business and grows revenues.

In fact, according to a study Etsy did in 2018, the time a maker spends on making their products is 52 percent. The remaining 48 percent is divided up between packaging and shipping products, managing inventory, purchasing supplies, and communicating with customers. According to the Etsy sellers in this study, they allocate only 9 percent of their total time for marketing and social media and 3 percent for planning for the future.

This means that as demand grows, most hobby owners just give up portions of the operating work and trade that time for production work because they get overwhelmed with filling orders. Or they end up working longer hours to make up for it—which must come from somewhere else in their lives. Then, when they feel like there is no longer a good "work/life balance," they try to hire those services out to someone else which reduces the net gains for the business.

The other mistake a hobby owner makes is not realizing that once they hire a clone, they will spend less time doing the craft work and more time doing the additional overhead work. See, when you hire a clone, you don't double your production—you might only increase it by 50 percent, but you did probably double your costs due to paying wages. Why didn't production double? Well, it's because your production time is reduced and replaced with management time—you have to oversee your new employee and what they are doing. Also, as the owner, you have to do extra marketing, extra estimates, extra bookkeeping, and whatever else can grow your sales so you can generate enough revenue to pay for your new employee and still pay yourself, assuming you are paying yourself. We'll come back to that last point again.

But, again, what many hobby owners do is ignore this extra work altogether, put their heads down, and just keep doing what they love and **hope** everyone finds out about their amazing product and everything will work out for the best. This is called "Hope Marketing and Business Management" and despite its lovely name, it's the least effective way to run a business.

So, for my hobby owners reading this book, you are going to have to ask yourself right now: "Am I in this to run a business that can change my life? Or am I just trying to make money to help offset the costs of my hobby?" Because if you really want to take your skills and passions and make them a fulfilling business, you must think like a mogul.

Now, this really is a tough one for my extremely talented hobby owner friends because I have seen some really gifted artists who make and do amazing things. What they want to do is to keep creating more than they need because it's an outlet and expression of themselves. They want to share this talent with the world. Trust me—I get that. But hobbies cost money, and as such, they end up being side hustles, forcing a woman to have a "real job" to pay for their affliction. And once a side hustle, always a side hustle, until you make the mind shifts I am talking about in this book.

Before any of you reading this who identify as a hobby owner get your feelings hurt and think I'm diminishing your craft or expertise in any way, I want to let you know that's not the case. I've been a maker-turned-mogul too.

At one time in my life, I was a work-at-home mom and sustainable design and policy consultant who, while getting a master's degree, decided to go out and invent a recycled-content countertop product. I went from a ten-by-ten-foot shed in my backyard to a full-scale manufacturing company with nationwide distribution in the span of about five years. While I loved doing the work of making my product, my goal was to prove out the concepts I imagined of solving many problems in communities around the world. And I couldn't do that with me making one handmade countertop at a time, so I had to also think pragmatically about the end-result I really wanted and not just about how much fun I had experimenting.

This is where I was different from day one from most makers—I always held two ideals in my mind together for the kind of business I wanted. One was how can I get my hands dirty and continue to be creative. And the other was how can I make these handmade products in a way that allows me to expand worldwide so that the social, economic, and environmental benefits of the product can be maximized to their fullest potential?

This was my **wicked question**.

See, many of us are trapped by black-and-white thinking and problem solving. Yes or no. This or that. You are with us or against us. That kind of thing. This line of thinking, called the "Tyranny of the OR" by Jim Collins in his 2004 book *Built to Last: Successful Habits of Visionary Companies*, revealed that successful businesses don't buy into dichotomous thinking but embrace what he called the "Genius of the AND."

How do you break from the idea that as you plan, you are forced to choose between two options? Well, you ask the delightfully delicious "wicked question"—how you can have both options! What makes it wicked is that you free yourself from how everyone else is problem solving, and, almost like magic, you are taken down an entirely different creative thinking path to solutions that don't require you to completely sacrifice something you really want. In my case, it was "How can I still have fun being a mad scientist AND achieve world-domination?"

What this means is if you want to take a hobby or any solo effort and turn it into a full-fledged business, using the "wicked question" mode of thinking can be helpful. Your answers may tease out a variety of ideas and solutions that won't rob you of the pleasure that doing your craft gives you and the ways to make money doing it.

So, to turn hobbies and side hustles into businesses, you must do an honest evaluation of the cost of your personal time spent with your craft and be willing to put a number on that time. That is because many times I have found that when *all* the time a maker/artist is counted for and divided into the money earned, she is being paid less than minimum wage. Later, I'll prove that to you.

But for now, think like a mogul and figure out the salary you are trying to earn from this business you want to start. Obviously, you are filling many roles in your company on day one, from CEO to janitor, and it can be hard to figure out exactly what you should be paying yourself. So, let's poke around at a few numbers to get a rough idea.

According to the US Bureau of Labor Statistics, in 2018, the median salary of women between the ages of thirty-five to fifty-four earned per year was $22 per hour or $45,552 a year. This is salary data across the board for all full-time working women and does not distinguish between job types or work experience, meaning it includes lower paying unskilled jobs blended in with higher paying corporate positions as well as self-employed women. However, men in this same data set earned more at $26 per hour or $54,080 a year.

Now, because I want you to think like a mogul, let's actually take a look at the numbers for business management. To find that out, you have to actually look at the Current Population Survey (CPS) done by the US Census Bureau. The latest figures there for 2019 showed that women in Management Occupations had a median income of $1,266 per week or $65,832 per year.

Want to know where men in the same category were? Well, the median income for men in the exact same 2019 survey was $1,659 per week or $86,268 per year. Bullshit, huh?

In fact, according to the statistics, women's median salaries were about 60–81 percent of men's salaries for the same positions, with the disparity growing in high-paying jobs. We are definitely going to talk about that more later, but for now, let's talk about what you are going to earn in your business and, Sis, you are not going to pay yourself less than what a man would give himself.

But another thought here before you pick your number and move on is that, if you are going to put the time and energy into this business of yours, think really hard about making it so that you can take care of yourself and your family if you need to. Or, right now, choose to approach this like a hobby instead and just know that if a crisis happens, like a death or divorce, that you will have to quit this business and get a higher paying job.

Why the doom and gloom? Because also according to our friends at the US Census Bureau, there are more single women and single mothers living in poverty than men. In fact, 25 percent of all single-parent households with no father present are in poverty. That means you should not set this business up to pay you minimum wage or less if you want to make an honest go at it because you never know if this business will be the only income you have. Trust me on this.

Your next business mogul move is to think about how much it would cost to hire someone to make your products for you or do your work. Why? Because we want to paint an accurate picture of what it costs to do your business plus give yourself room to let you be your company's CEO and have your work still going on at the same time. Additionally, it's feasible that to get the salary you want, you need to produce a higher volume than what you can do on your own. We don't know yet, and we might come back to this number later and change it once we look at the data during exercises later in this book. For now, I would use $22 per hour as the budget.

No. Fuck that. Remember, we're ending the gender salary gap right now, so budget $26 per hour. Yes, that's better.

The bottom line is that your business goals must be about the bottom line. You must be driven to create a business that will make enough money to help you get to the destination you want. If, however, you are content with making just enough to cover your costs of your hobby, that is okay too. But remember that your hobby will cost you more in the long run if you mistake what you are doing for operating a full-scale business. In a very sneaky way, your hobby could be draining your finite resources like your time and money and sabotaging your future. And it might be less costly overall to simply budget a line item out of your household expenses for your hobby and just let it be what it is. And trust me, we are definitely going to talk about this fully in another chapter.

So, what I want you to do is go through the following series of questions and think about your answer to them. The point is to see if you nail down your true motivations for why you are, at this point in your life, looking to become an entrepreneur.

EXERCISE

1. When did you first think about owning your own business? What was happening at the time?

2. Are you motivated by the idea that self-employment will give you freedom? How do you define this freedom? More time? More money?

3. Do you have a particular goal or problem you want to solve?

4. Is money a motivating factor for why you want to start your own business? If not, why?

5. Do you want to make more money than you are making right now? If so, how much?

6. Are you now where you want to be financially? Is this causing you any pain in your life?

7. What does financial freedom look like for you? What does that mean?

YOUR ULTIMATE DESTINATION

Okay, now are you ready to let the rubber hit the road and sit down and figure out why you really want to do this. What is the lifestyle you really want to have? That idea is a big part of the endgame here. In fact, it **is** the destination. There will be no more of this work-life balance BS everyone is used to hearing about. The only reason people talk about it so much is because they are driving a car around the block over and over again, trading one hour of their day for a dollar, going nowhere. So of course, they need something else that is fulfilling. But that's not what we are doing here, remember? We are planning a trip and we're going to make sure you have fun during the journey to the lifestyle you want.

So, at this point, sit at your desk or big comfy chair or wherever you can think clearly and without interruption, and put these next thoughts into writing. But I want you to not just lock the door to your room and keep your friends, kids, and partners out—lock the door in your head and keep out all of the voices that will argue and debate with you and tell you that you can't do this, whatever "this" is.

The next destination-setting exercise is about setting yourself free because there are no rules you need to follow. Don't worry about solving it as you go. Don't worry about whether what you want has been done before by people you know. And don't worry if someone else thinks you can't or shouldn't do this. Just close your eyes and imagine yourself at some real point in the future with the life you really want to have.

If you are like me, with teenagers who will both be graduated and out on their own in the next five years, then use five years from today. If you have small children and your vision of the ultimate goal is further out, then think of that. Or, if you want to have this new life while your children are young because it's motivating to think of having free time to spend with them, that's okay too. Again, there are no rules except that I want you to choose a real date and then time-travel there.

EXERCISE

1.   What kind of home or environment are you living in? Describe the details you see and want in your mind.
2.   What does your typical day look like? What are you doing? How are you spending your time?

3. What is your role in your business? Are you working all day or part-time?
4. Do you have a fixed office with lots of employees? Or is your work environment flexible and mobile?
5. Now, create the perfect lifestyle and business that blends with it—describe what that is.

Now, dig deep and then ask yourself "why" you really want all these things.

1. Why do I really want this lifestyle?
2. What is my ultimate goal?
3. What is the outcome from this goal that makes me want it?
4. And why do I want that outcome?

I have to ask you—as you visualized all this, could you feel it? I mean, did you smile uncontrollably? Did your heart race a little with excitement like you were actually experiencing all of this? I hope so! Because if you did, then you just got your taste of the biggest secret of all—once you feel it and want it and realize how good it will be for you to have it, nothing will stop you from working toward it.

WHO'S COMING WITH YOU

Before we end this chapter, I want to bring up a cautionary tale that affects more would-be women entrepreneurs than men. Ever been on a vacation with someone who hated it and complained about it the whole time? Yeah, I think we all have. And how did that go for you? Yeah, it sucked. Either you're pulling someone along who is dragging their feet and slowing you down. Or they try to rewrite the itinerary that you've carefully planned out because they think they have better ideas. And in the worst cases, someone gets sick and the whole trip gets called off or shortened. As much as I hate being cold, I hate group trips because I hate having a plan for how I want to enjoy my vacation and feel pressured to compromise with people who don't have the same outcomes in mind.

Sure, compromise is a part of life, but there are circumstances where you must remember that it is okay to choose your needs over someone else's wants. And sometimes that need is to live your true life of authenticity. You are allowed that, despite what people told you growing up.

But some of you do have a group to think about. It's your spouse, partner, or maybe even small children. So, I will say this as directly as necessary: I hope to god that they are on the same page with you because I've seen too many women, including myself, forestall their own ambitions so as to not break a connection with their spouse or partner.

In fact, in 2004, Pamela Stone and Meg Lovejoy, two researchers on women in the workforce, released a study called "Fast-Track Women and the 'Choice' to Stay Home." Looking to see if women were quitting their careers because they viewed themselves as "new traditionalists"—that is, they believed full-time motherhood took precedence over careers, the researchers found something else was happening.

They discovered that two-thirds of the women sampled in the study cited their husbands as a key influence in why they gave up their careers to become stay-at-home moms. And the central reasons were around the idea that a woman's role was taking all the material and emotional labors of parenting. One woman in the study was quoted as saying "My husband has always said to me, 'You can do whatever you want to do.' But he's not there to pick up any load." This study even observed that women with high-status jobs who earned more than their husbands were persuaded to defer to their husband's preference for the woman to bear the brunt of family work. This placed these women in a double-bind of feeling like they had to "choose" their family over their own careers. In the end, no matter what lip service husbands gave to supporting their wives' careers, that support rarely included being available to share the "second-career" efforts of the family.

Since 2004, marriages have no longer been just between heterosexual couples, and while there may be some career-stifling wives in same-sex marriages out there, the vast majority of these issues come from the gender imbalances we still see in society today.

In fact, even in 2020, as the pandemic forced the closure of childcare businesses and schools, a staggering number of women left their careers or cut back on their hours to stay at home. According the US Census Bureau's data, three times as many women changed or left their jobs than men. And by the looks of commentary on social media, not all of them were happy about that. But if someone is expected to make personal and professional sacrifices, we still assume it's all on the women to do it.

Now, if children are not a factor in your life, that may be helpful, but it doesn't mean you won't have to contend with the same underlying beliefs that a man's career and role in the family unit has more weight than the woman's and that it's his career that sets the destination for the family.

If that is the case in your family and with your spouse, there are no easy answers to this problem. I can't recommend what you should do if you are not supported at home to put this business together. But I can tell you that something will have to give if you both don't share the same values and investment in the success of your venture. You will have a very hard decision ahead of you. So, if it seems that there is a misalignment, I do encourage you to open up the doors of communication early and wide so that you both have a chance to express your feelings.

To get your partner onboard, it's important that you are able to share your ultimate goals and motives with them because if they are the same for them or they can benefit from them, then they are more likely to be supportive of the work you have ahead of you.

But if your goal is to travel a lot, for example, and they only see that as a threat to their own career or ambition, you are going to have some serious misalignments. That introduces the possibilities of sabotaging behaviors by you or your partner. Having a thoughtful conversation with your partner may include employing several wicked questions as you sort this out, depending on the concerns or challenges you have.

"IT'S TIME FOR ME TO GET IT RIGHT"

Elizabeth, a life coach and speaker in the Seattle area, has tackled the issue of her ambitions versus her partner's not once, but twice so far in her life. Married for twenty-one years and divorced in 2016, Elizabeth had to come to terms with the fact that her husband's beliefs about marriage and roles were going to keep her from fulfilling her true passions and talents.

Like many men and women who are looking at ending a long marriage, this was not an easy decision to come to. In fact, Elizabeth's first steps were to see if the marriage could be preserved under new terms. But over the course of twenty-one years, the marriage dissolved regardless. She attributes that to when she started a nonprofit helping woman find their way back from poverty and domestic violence. When it all began, her ex supported her work publicly, but in private, her work and the time she spent in homeless shelters with these women created conflict in their marriage.

When Elizabeth and I talked about where her ex's beliefs about marriage came from, Elizabeth said she thought it was the direct result of his own family life. His own mother was a teacher and left her career to be home with the children. So, when Elizabeth had her first child while happily working as a systems administrator for a large company, her ex "informed me that one of us needed to be home to take care of the children, and obviously, that was me."

Elizabeth did take a sabbatical from her career to raise the kids, but deep inside, while she did love her role as Mom, she had that inner pull that told her she was created for more, which prompted her to start her nonprofit in 2000. Employing the concept of the wicked question, Elizabeth felt she had set the structure up in a way that she could be Mom and wife and help women through her nonprofit. Her ex, however, still found the intrusion to be too much. It brought up his own insecurities into their marriage, leading to the end of the relationship.

Now single, Elizabeth ventured back into entrepreneurship when she opened a dress shop in 2017. Unintentionally, having women come into the store rekindled her passion for helping women rebuild their lives. When the customers would come in for their personal styling help, Elizabeth found herself naturally being drawn into coaching and offering advice and she realized that's what she was meant for.

A wiser, more experienced woman than when she got married over two decades ago, Elizabeth found herself in a new eight-month-old relationship with a man who she was hopeful would make a better partner. This hopefulness was based in part that when she originally shared her vision of her path forward, he was very excited about it. Unfortunately, when she started to do the work and take the actions to bring it all to life, the pushbacks began. She also sensed that familiar third wheel of insecurity intruding into the relationship through his statements like, "I don't know where I can fit in to all this." And this became her first red flag that this relationship might not pass the strength, mutuality, and sustainability tests.

"At the beginning, this person would tell me he supported me and wanted to see me doing really well at my work. But then it turned into things like I'm working on my website to get my new business up and running, and I had asked for this quiet time and space to get it done. Only, I would be constantly interrupted and then the accusations of not giving him enough attention would follow. And I'm responding with 'Wait a minute—you're not a toddler and you know I slotted this time to work on this.'"

Sadly, as is often the case for people, her partner's defense of his actions was because he said he loved her. But instead, it felt to her more like control, and she wasn't interested in a partnership like that again. The person she met originally evaporated and the real man appeared. Shortly thereafter, she ended the relationship.

The conclusion that Elizabeth came to was that while the man she was seeing had some beautiful qualities, he had not yet started doing any of the hard work required to address the other things in his life that needed attention. And she had to remind herself of the same message she delivered at her workshops. And after allowing that to happen to her in the past, Elizabeth, like many other women, is just not going to allow it anymore.

She continues, "I'm fifty-four years old. It's time for me to get it right, especially if I'm asking other women to get it right, and that's what I plan to do."

So, listen—I know there are amazing partners, husbands, and wives out there who have secure relationships with themselves and with their spouses. I just don't know what *your* relationship is like, so I'm just trying to be real with you about what I have seen that has thwarted some really smart women and their attempts to be successfully self-employed.

Some couples do well as business partners, but most don't and the differences are in the strength in communication between the two of them, if they have the same mindsets regarding failures and growth, and if they can give each other the gift of listening.

I have coached women who really want their spouse to be their business partner in their own company, thinking that working together will bring closeness. Unfortunately, if the spouse does not share the same enthusiasm for the work or becomes insecure due to the attention the woman is paying toward her career versus them, or they feel that her success will be emasculating, they can actually strangle any good intentions of the business or aspirations their wife or partner has.

Now, given that I have spent enough of my own time sharing my bedroom and boardroom with the main man in my life, I know that mixing business and relationships is very risky. Especially since you have to be willing to challenge the other person, at times, for the sake of the business. Therefore, being business partners has a strong likelihood of introducing a power-struggle and a potentially damaging third wheel into your relationship.

However, I do believe it's possible that a spouse could occasionally be tapped to help out as an employee, so long as your authority is respected and they perform the services you need. It can be fun working together on a project or a task for your business. Plus, a caring, supportive partner *wants* to show you that they believe in you and are willing to give you a hand with whatever they can, so finding a way to include them can be good for your relationship if you have well-set boundaries.

In the end, we should all have our own endeavors and outlets because it allows that full, uninhibited expression of who we are as individuals to blossom with no one else's hands fouling it up. This provides you with complete autonomy and should anything catastrophic happen between you and your spouse, you don't risk losing your business and your source of income. And to be honest, a secure, respectful relationship with another person has room for you to do your thing professionally on your own, as long as you are meeting the emotional needs of your partner and vice versa.

But, despite my warnings, if you do decide to become business partners with your spouse, I encourage you both to establish a clear set of guidelines and rules to honor about how business conflicts will be handled and how decisions will be made—including who gets the final call when you are at an impasse. If your partner is resistant or insulted by suggestions, this is a red flag you should heed. Don't be persuaded by the idea that you can "figure it out as you go" or by the romantic idea that you love each other, and you'll find a way. No—leave the romance out of the business and think like a mogul bringing on *any* business partner—work out a plan and put it into writing. No exceptions.

And, finally, whether you like it or not, have a clear exit plan for the business in the event of a divorce. It's easier to negotiate this early than in the heat and pain of a separation, which is exactly why prenuptial agreements exist! And this is a tragic lesson I learned the hard way.

So, here's the last step to complete if you have a spouse or partner to help make sure you are both in alignment with reasons you have for pursuing entrepreneurship.

EXERCISE

1. How would our family roles and responsibilities need to change if I pursue this path?
2. What are the mutual benefits of me doing this?
3. What are my partner's/spouse's concerns?
4. Do my goals align with my partner's personal goals? If not, in what ways?
5. What changes can we make now to make some of the goals more attainable?

Now, I'm warning you: I'm going to make you return to your reflections from this entire chapter many times as we continue through this book. So, I encourage you to be brave and thoughtful about what you write down and imagine for yourself. I will also say that it's going to be okay if, after you keep reading and learning more about yourself as we go along here, you come back here and change your reason "Why" even more. If you don't quite yet understand the impact of knowing your destination before you start your business, you will as you continue.

The point of this chapter isn't about putting your business and dreams into numbers. It's about tapping into the deepest core reasons you are looking to change and how this business can help you do that.

...

Chapter Three

YOUR BRAIN AND YOUR BUSINESS

> *"The brain is wider than the sky."*

–Emily Dickinson

You might be entering this chapter on the high of the last one, which is wonderful. However, as your friend, I can't let you continue on without the most important component to answering your question about how to start a business.

Remember, anyone can start a business, but not everyone will stay in business. And yes, there is a huge piece related to what you want to do with your business and where you are going. In other words, your reasons "why." But, at the risk of over-using the driving analogy a bit more, we all also know that if we can't drive a car or read a road map, it doesn't matter where we want to go and how badly we want to go there, we'll never make it.

So, that's why it is really important to start to talk about you, the driver. And in this chapter, I'm going to present things you have probably never heard or realized before as it relates to business and business success. This is the beginning of all the things I wish I knew before I started my own adventures in entrepreneurship.

SKILLS TO SUCCEED IN BUSINESS

Over the years, I noticed that there are major skills a business owner must have, and these are like the legs on a three-legged stool. Sometimes, my clients hire me because they are usually trying to address one problem for their business, and I can actually see that they are sitting on a wobbly stool. And so, for people who want to succeed and thrive in business, being balanced in all three of the following skills is critical.

ORGANIZATION & PLANNING

The first leg or skillset is organization and planning. These skills involve not just having the ability to develop the long-range business goals, but they also include the ability to turn those goals into actual actions and to follow through on them.

The skills that are mission-critical on a day-to-day level include the following:

- Setting goals or priorities and then coming up with the tasks or actions you must take to meet them.

- Keeping important details or paperwork organized and current.
- Maintaining focus and minimizing distractions.

Now, when we have to pull back and take a broader viewpoint of our business, we also need to be able to do these activities:

- Establish long-term goals or plans that may take one, two, or even five years to reach.
- Consistently review these plans and check in to see if you are on track.
- Be able to forecast or predict how long it will take to reach milestones that may be a few months in the future.

Between these two lists, I have seen many entrepreneurs possess a real strength in one but not the other. On one end, I've met lots of "business planners" or visionaries who get incredibly energized from the big ideas and from setting long-term targets and goals for their business. But they often have problems being motivated to do the "less exciting," more mundane daily work needed to meet their goals. Their eyes are always on the horizon, scanning and looking for the next cool direction to go while not watching what their feet are doing.

And then there are those who start a business and labor meticulously over every fine detail, like what color to paint the walls in their office to maximize their creativity. Or they furiously bury their heads into the day-to-day but haven't thought about where they want to be in a couple of months or years. This person is walking along the road of entrepreneurship looking at the ground directly underneath them, watching each step, forgetting to look up, and then accidentally walking straight into a light pole. That's why the real mastery of this skillset is to have a powerful desire to do both.

LEADERSHIP & PEOPLE SKILLS

The next leg of the stool of entrepreneurship is leadership and people skills. Even if you never want employees, this is vital. That is because we are always engaging and interacting with other people in many forms such as how we conduct meetings and how we speak through email, the phone, or on social media.

Leadership and people skills include the following:

- Being able to pick up on emotional or social cues and adapting as needed in conversations.
- Having confidence to tackle and discuss uncomfortable topics in a constructive manner.
- Using persuasion and influence to have others do what you need in marketing or sales.
- Having an ability to form connections quickly with people you don't know and gain their trust.

Again, you don't have to have employees to appreciate the importance of this skillset. Your customers are people. Your suppliers are people. The people you network with are people. Therefore, if you lack the drive to want to understand how to form powerful connections with other people and to leverage those connections for the purposes of your businesses, your business may languish in anonymity, no matter how great your product or service is.

Here's the big thing to know, if you are shy or insecure about your people skills, if you just want to ignore that as a businesswoman, and if you aren't convincing and confident about your product or service, you are going to be a chronic underearner, which leads us to the third leg of our stool.

FINANCIAL MANAGEMENT

We all know that businesses that don't make money don't stick around for very long. So, obviously, going into business and not being financially literate is a surefire way to lose before you even begin. The thing about money is that it's not as easy as understanding dollars and cents. It is a complicated topic that many people struggle with because one needs to know more than how to balance a checkbook.

Having full financial literacy also means the following:

- Knowing how to pay your bills on time and avoiding the costs of late fees and penalties.
- Setting budgets based on actual expenses and needs and sticking to them.
- Being able to forecast spending, income fluctuations, and sales targets.
- Understanding how to set a proper price for your product or service that allows you to meet financial goals.

See, most of us know math pretty well and have the basic financial literacy to begin our own businesses. It's the other, underlying things we don't understand that trip us up. More about that later too.

WHY DO BUSINESSES FAIL?

Before we get to the heart of this chapter, I want to talk about why businesses fail. And let me clarify why this is important: it's because businesses don't actually fail on their own; it's the people who start them and decide for one reason or another that they can't continue on.

First, a lot of businesses manage to make it through the hard, cold winter of their first year. In fact, when the Small Business Administration's Office of Advocacy published their data in 2019, they found that four out of five businesses started in 2017 actually made it until 2018 and that this was pretty similar to the survival rates for the entire ten years prior. So, the odds are pretty good that you will be a business owner for at least a year, pandemics notwithstanding.

But then, trends over several years show that only about **half of all** businesses will last at least five years. And then, only one-third of all businesses will make it to ten years.

So, what happens in those first five years? CB Insights is a private company that provides market and business intelligence to other companies. In 2019, they reviewed more than a hundred start-up post-mortems by former business owners to find out the reasons why their businesses closed. As they sifted through the answers, they found several themes and compiled a list of the top twenty reasons.

- No market need: 42 percent
- Ran out of cash: 29 percent
- Wrong team: 23 percent
- Outcompeted: 19 percent
- Pricing or cost issues: 18 percent
- Unfriendly user product: 17 percent
- Product without a business model: 17 percent
- Poor marketing: 14 percent
- Ignored customers: 14 percent
- Mistimed product: 13 percent
- Lost focus: 13 percent
- Disharmony among team and/or investors: 13 percent
- Pivot gone bad: 10 percent
- Lack of passion: 9 percent
- Failed geographical expansion: 9 percent
- No financing or investor interest: 8 percent
- Legal challenges: 8 percent
- Didn't use network: 8 percent
- Burned out: 8 percent
- Failure to pivot: 7 percent

Looking at the top three reasons, you can see that they look eerily like the company did not have strong skills in the basics that I just ran you through, don't they? In fact, the list has several reasons that could be tossed into one of those three buckets of planning, leadership, and financial know-how.

That's why I believe these reasons are the **results** of having some deep-seated issues.

Because what's interesting about these figures is that the rates of failure are consistent throughout the years, even during economic downturns. That is, even during the Recession and the years that followed, small business failure rates didn't skyrocket. They remained steady, suggesting that economic factors don't have as significant an impact on the success of small business survival as many may think. That tells me there is something else that's happening. Because, again, businesses don't fail—people do.

Now, self-help wouldn't be about an eleven billion dollar a year industry if there was a magic bullet out there for solving all our problems. The facts are that the solutions that work best for people are as varied as the people are. But it's frustrating when you can't seem to figure out how to get yourself off the ground and successfully reach the goals that you really do want. So, now it's time to learn what is really going on.

THE TRUTH ABOUT OUR BRAINS

First, forget the myth that our brains are completely formed when we're born, and so if we have "emotional problems" or "mental health issues," that is only because we got a bad model. This old idea is at the heart of treatments and stigmas surrounding mental health. Our viewpoints about "mental illnesses" in society keep people closeted in shame.

In fact, the next time you need a pick-me-up in the form of a Channing Tatum movie, go find the 2009 masterpiece *G.I. Joe: The Rise of Cobra* and in it you will hear one of the characters, Scarlett, played by Rachel Nichols, state, "Emotions are not based on science. And if you can't quantify or prove that something exists, well, then in my mind, it doesn't."

But today, when we take about forty years of psychology studies and link it with about twenty years of research into neuroscience and neurobiology, there is evidence that emotions are, in fact, biological and that they aren't uncontrollable or unsolvable mysteries. Also, our responses and behaviors to situations aren't the luck of the genetic draw either. Remember nature **and** nurture.

Grasping this one thing—the fact that the science is there and the fact that it's not well-known or has reached a saturation point in our society is exactly why I started to podcast and become a mental health advocate. Bringing this knowledge to the field of business was important to me because I knew that this information would change the lives of many people, especially women.

THE FIRST YEARS: BRAIN BUILDING

Up until now, when researchers and scientists wanted to understand human behavior, they had to study animals. But since imaging technology is available, such as MRIs, CAT scans, and now the more powerful magnetoencephalography or MEG scans, science can non-invasively see inside the human brain and measure changes on a millisecond-by-millisecond basis. This technology, along with significant advances in computers and software, not to mention the complete mapping of the human genome in 2003, have all blown the doors off of what we thought we knew about our bodies and our brains.

In my quest to better understand neuroscience, aside from all the journals and books I could read, I reached out to the Institute for Learning & Brain Sciences (I-LABS) at the University of Washington and got a chance to be further educated by Dr. Amelia Bachleda. One of her roles is to take the complex world of neurobiology and distill it into bite-sized, easy to understand concepts for the rest of us. And since many of you reading this are probably not neuroscientists, I want to make sure we are laying out an important primer on how the organic computers and software programs in our bodies work twenty-four hours a day, seven days week. Because despite the desire to flip switches between your "normal brain" and "business brain"— it's all one brain.

So, to begin, one thing that research in the field of neuroscience has revealed is that there are two really distinct and important phases of brain development. And for my readers who are parents, I want you to read through this next section and imagine yourself not as a parent, but as the child being parented, so that it can hopefully make more sense to you as an adult today.

First, when we are born, our brain is only about 25 percent of the size it will be when we are adults, but we are actually born with almost all of the brain cells or neurons that we will ever need. These neurons are the special types of cells that form the complex communication network we have throughout our brains. The catch, however, is that aside from basic core functions, most of the synapses, which are the real physical connections between these cells, are not wired together yet.

But by the age of five, our brains are about 95 percent of our adult size, which tells us there is a ton of growth that happens. However, 95 percent of adult size does not mean 95 percent developed, which is obvious if you've ever hung out with a five-year-old. Now, the most astonishing thing is that between birth and about three years old, the brain is soaking up an extraordinary amount of information and the largest amount of the neural wiring is actually happening before the age of three. In fact, scientists estimate that there are **1,000,000 million connections being made per second** during this time period.

So, if you need something a little more concrete to understand what is happening, then think of brain architecture like constructing a home. From birth to five years old, 95 percent of the house is built: the walls are up, the floors and the ceilings are in, all the light switches and the light fixtures are installed, and how this house looks is based on the DNA that we've inherited.

But what's missing is the copper wiring between all the lights and switches. That wiring is just lying there on the ground or hanging loose in the walls and ceilings but isn't connected. The Electrician needs to be told what to do and so that's where the experiences we have comes to play. Our childhood experiences teach the Electrician where to put the copper wiring and which lights will come on when certain switches are flipped.

Amelia adds, "I might even go to the extent of we're not quite sure which lights need to come on yet, you know? Because maybe we're not sure how we're going to use that house. So, we might not know what areas are going to need more light, which areas will need less light, and when do those lights need to turn on and off?"

And how does the electrician get the information to do the wiring? Well, researchers and scientists believe there is a specific strategy for how these experiences translate into the connections in our brains. This process is called **serve and return**.

According to the Center on the Developing Child at Harvard University, "serve and return" is like the back and forth of a game of tennis or ping-pong. Much like lobbing a ball over the net to the player on the other side of the court, an infant or child does something to get an adult's attention, like babble, make a face or cry (the serve). If the other player, in this case, an adult, responds appropriately through making eye contact, speaking back or hugging, the metaphorical ball is returned, and a neural connection is being wired or strengthened.

"Children are born wanting to have this social interaction," according to Amelia. "One of the earlier studies that showed this was done by one of I-LABS co-directors, Dr. Andrew Melton, in the 1970s. And what he basically did was go to hospitals and, with the parent's permission, made faces at newborn babies. He stuck his tongue out. He opened his mouth. He made faces that newborn babies can physically make. And sure enough many babies within hours of being born made those facial expressions right back at him. This is one of the studies that really started to shift the field of developmental psychology by saying that children are born wanting to be a part of a conversation. Long before a child knows what a tongue is or a mouth is or who you are, they really are born ready, like biologically ready, to start having that back-and-forth interaction that we know is so fundamentally important for child development."

Because the back-and-forth interaction is essential to brain architecture, when it doesn't happen at all or the responses are unreliable or inappropriate, research is seeing that development of these neural connections is disrupted and in turn leads to possible physical, mental, and emotional health impairment.

In fact, the ongoing absence of serve and return, that is, a child's attempts to connect with their primary caregiver—or any adult, really—are not answered or returned, the child's stress response then gets activated and the developing brain is getting a double whammy of poor interactions along with being flooded with harmful stress hormones, which we'll come back to later.

But why does the brain do this, activate the alarm system in the child's body? Because that is how important these connections are for not only surviving but actually thriving. To humans, these connections are a matter of life and death. So, if serve and return is not happening for a child or is done so inconsistently and inappropriately, the brain begins to sense danger, more particularly that if the child cannot make a stable connection with the adult, the child could die. Now, it's obvious an infant will perish without food and shelter but only in the last twenty to thirty years did researchers begin to uncover the evidence that emotional connections were just as important.

Following the fall of the Romanian dictatorship in 1989, people around the world began to learn that there were over 150,000 children being raised in deplorable conditions within the country's orphanages. This prompted a team of psychologists from the United States to travel and study the situation.

Right away, they found that the babies' basic needs were being met, such as being fed, diapered, and bathed on a schedule, but that was it. They were left to lie in their cribs alone all day, and what the research team noticed was that the babies barely cried. No one ever answered them, picked them up, and held these babies in their arms, looked into their faces and spoke to them, or engaged with them. And as the children grew older, they continued to live and be treated like tiny castaways. The severity of this was obvious.

Throughout the fourteen-year study, what the researchers found was that not only did the children who lived exclusively in the orphanage have severe delays in their cognitive function, but, through the use of MRIs, it was seen that the physical sizes of their brains were also smaller. They had lower volume in gray matter, which is primarily the neurons, and white matter, which is the nerve fibers or synapses that connect the neurons together. In other words, they have smaller houses, with fewer lights and wires between them. Without an electrician, the children were left to try to figure this out as much as they could on their own. So, without the brain-building interactions of serve and return, these poor children grew up in an environment that was terrifying, unnatural, and toxic. And they suffered for it.

ADOLESCENT YEARS: PRUNING & REINFORCING

We know some of the obvious things children learn while growing up, like how to talk, walk, feed themselves, use a bathroom, not eat bugs, et cetera, but what is the brain also learning during the serve and return interactions between a child and an adult? Well, the biggest ones are the skills known as **executive function** and **self-regulation**.

Executive function is defined by the American Psychology Association as the suite of "...higher level cognitive processes of planning, decision-making, problem solving, action sequencing, task assignment and organization, effortful and persistent goal pursuit, inhibition of competing impulses, flexibility in goal selection, and goal-conflict resolution."

In other words, we are talking about short term memory, mental flexibility, self-control, and how well these functions all work together. So, if we are successfully applying our executive function capabilities in real life, it means that we can:

- Retain, access, and process information over short periods of time (pay attention and remember, in other words).
- Sustain and shift our attentions easily in response to different demands without becoming overwhelmed. Or we can see that different situations call for different rules or actions.
- Exercise self-control so that we can set priorities and resist impulsive actions or responses.

These are the major mental processes that we rely on for planning, focus, and memory and give us the ability to keep many balls up on the air at once successfully. If these skills are well developed, we are the kind of adult who knows how to set priorities, not be derailed by distractions, plan, set, and achieve goals, and not be carried away by impulsive behavior, all critical in regular life and in entrepreneurial life.

Again, we now know we were not born with these skills. We were born with the *potential to develop them*. If we had opportunities through our experiences to learn them from the adults in our lives, obviously we are then gifted with the abilities to make healthy choices for ourselves and contribute positively to society. But if we did not get what our developing brains needed from our relationships with the key adults in our lives, these skills may be delayed or impaired to some extent.

Now, after the brain has formed a mind-boggling number of connections from the moment of birth through our young years, there is another distinct phase of brain development that starts at about eleven years old and, believe it or not, actually doesn't end until we are about twenty-five years old. It's called the **adolescent brain development** phase.

Because our brains want to be efficient, researchers believe that, at this time, our brains are starting to decide on all the connections it formed, which ones are important to keep (blooming) and which ones to get rid of (pruning). And this is done by the brain keeping track of the experiences and interactions we have, good and bad, and storing those so that the brain can access the right response in the future. That last sentence is important to remember.

But it is during this period that the part of the brain where executive function resides, the prefrontal cortex, is also becoming more developed. A brain more fitting for adulthood is forming.

Thanks to researchers, parents now have explanations for why teenagers behave and frustrate us the way they do—because while they look like adults or are the same physical size as an adult, they simply don't have the executive function of the brains we as adults have.

So, they make bad decisions. They can't stay focused. But most importantly—memory is affected, and they forget things—a lot! And while frustrating, this is completely normal and an incredibly complex process of rewiring the brain that, again, we have only recently discovered is going on inside our heads.

That's why, during this phase of brain architecture development, it is important that teens can make choices and decisions on their own, even if they are dumb ones. Forcing decisions onto them can impede their executive function development. Since the brain needs to learn from experiences, challenging your teen's decisions all the time and forcing them to do what you think they need to do interferes with the brain's own programming. Telling our kids what to do all the time robs them of understanding an important part of decision-making and priority-setting which is **cause and effect**. That is, their brains don't get to learn from the good and bad consequences of their choices.

As a parent of two teenagers myself, I fully get the desire to spare our kids from dumb decisions and the tendency to get very dictatorial with them at this phase instead of giving them freedom. We already know what the right choice might be based on our own experience and want to help our kids skip the "learning the hard way" steps. But now we know that's the wrong thing to do.

See, when parents are constantly demanding or always questioning every action or choice a teenager makes in a harsh and judgmental way, it can become disruptive to their developing brain. This in turn may lead to some kids having greater difficulty with focus and follow through because instead of forming solutions in their heads, they hear the angry voice of the parent raising doubts. This teen then may not know what to do next because they are questioning every thought in their head instead of acting.

Parenting during the teenage years is, without a doubt, ridiculously hard. We think going in after years of temper tantrums, changing diapers, and sleepless nights that parenting will be easier once they are older, but it's not. It's simply different because adolescent brain development is also when teens are going to behave in riskier activities and start to individuate from their parents (again, a completely natural thing for them to do). And many parents have difficulties with who they see as a defiant, obstinate, and ungrateful child, and tensions in the house can increase.

So, remember the earlier discussion on family roles and differentiation? The power struggles related to roles start to emerge heavily during this phase as well because some parents use these definitions of roles as the guidelines for grooming their child into what they think they need to be rather than who the teenager is blossoming into on their own. Knowing this, I think it's important that we all reflect on our own teenage years and see if we can't remember some of the issues we may have had during this time with our family and if we can still hear the arguments ringing in our ears from back then.

Finally, another important element of how the brain works and grows is to understand that it doesn't happen in little pockets in isolation from one another. So, while the executive functions all live in the frontal lobe and the prefrontal cortex, all areas of our brain are working at the same time. And as a result, despite our desire to be focusing on work or a task, if some other part of the brain is stimulated due to a stressor or danger signal going off, it can interfere with our abilities to do that.

Amelia explains, "The frontal lobe region is really important for the executive functioning skills but at the same time, they're networked with all of these different regions of the brain. Which is why we can have experiences when we're really startled or afraid or anxious and where we're not thinking as clearly so we might not be as able to focus on a task. That tells us that part of the brain might not be as active, and we might be sort of using some of those other regions of our brain."

In other words, if your brain senses any danger, you're screwed.

BRAIN-BUILDING POISON: FEAR & TOXIC STRESS

So, how does the brain do this—protect us from danger?

By making us feel afraid.

Do you get that? Let me say this again for the people in the back because this is really important: If the primary objective of the human brain's program is to keep us alive, then it means fear is the primary motivational tool used by our brains.

And how is this feeling of fear triggered in us by our super-efficient brain? It is done through the internal alarm system in our brains called the acute stress response or, more commonly, **fight-or-flight**.

Truth be told, before we dive in here, I have to get on my soapbox and let you know that one of the most annoying things I hear is when people refer to this response mechanism as some sort of useless primitive function that is left over from caveman days and serves no purpose today. You've probably heard people talk about is as "We only needed it back when we had to watch out for saber-toothed tigers."

But that's not true! Our fight-or-flight function is not like extra wisdom teeth in our mouths or piles of useless body hair. We are still confronted with danger every day. And while it's sometimes called the "primitive" parts of our brains—that does **not** mean it's antiquated or unintelligent.

What is means is that the areas of the brain where this work is done is the oldest part of the human brain, in terms of evolution, and it's the first parts to form during development. So, that makes fight-or-flight the most experienced part of our neurological system and really, *really* efficient and effective at its job.

And guess what? This system gets activated probably more often than you realize, especially in the stressful world of business, because we think of danger as an adult as specific, easy to identify life-threatening situations and don't always realize that alarms are being pulled and our bodies are in high-alert mode. But the reality is the danger signals our brain uses to alert us were designed when we were children!

It works like this: When someone confronts danger like an oncoming car, an ominous dark alley, or the weird look on another person's face, the eyes or ears (or both) send the information to the amygdala, an area of the brain that contributes to emotional processing. The amygdala interprets the images and sounds and if it senses something that it perceives as danger, it instantly sends a distress signal to the hypothalamus.

But wait—first, how does the amygdala know what "danger" is, you might ask? Are dangerous scenarios preprogrammed into our brains? Nope. Not all of them. We learn what danger is from our traumatic experiences. And while trauma has many definitions, typically in psychology it refers to an experience of serious adversity or terror—or the emotional or psychological response to that experience. In other words, if what happened to you **as a child scared you**—no matter what it was—your little body and brain read that as traumatic and programmed that memory into your brain to use as a future reference. Period.

Also, obviously, things you did that caused your body extreme pain or if you witnessed the hurting or scaring of other people also got programmed for the amygdala to use as future data.

It's why you touched a hot stove or walked up to a growling dog only *one time* before your brain understood what that meant—don't do that again or you could die.

So, now that your amygdala has sensed something that it remembered as scary, possibly dangerous, and has raised the red flag to your hypothalamus, this tiny region at your brain's base, sets off an alarm system in your body. This alarm is **fear** and it is a bona fide biological process, causing a cascade of nerve and hormonal signals, prompting your adrenal glands, located atop your kidneys, to release a surge of hormones including adrenaline and cortisol through your body.

Adrenaline increases your heart rate, elevates your blood pressure, and boosts energy supplies. Cortisol, the primary stress hormone, increases sugars (glucose) in the bloodstream, enhances your brain's use of glucose and increases the availability of substances that repair tissues. This is so your muscles can work really fast at either running for your life or fighting back.

But cortisol also curbs functions that would be nonessential or detrimental in a fight-or-flight situation, saving those resources for surviving in the moment. It changes immune system responses and suppresses the digestive system, the reproductive system, and other processes. Ever noticed when you were in extreme stress that you didn't have much of an appetite or that you had zero sex drive?

How do we know our stress response has clicked on? Well, what do you feel like when you're afraid? For me, my heart pounds instantly and my chest might tighten up a bit too. But also, depending on the situation, I might feel a rise in anger because my natural stress response is "fight" and in order to want to conquer whatever it is that poses a danger to me, I can't really be in a state of love and compassion, can I? Nope. I need to feel feelings of hate and anger toward the adversary in front of me so that I can make the primitive and necessary life-and-death decisions to survive.

Now, the body's fight-or-flight system is usually self-limiting, meaning you don't have to tell it to shut off or worry about committing acts of murder every time someone looks at you the wrong way or criticizes your t-shirt. So, generally once a perceived threat has passed, your brain applies the brakes, and hormone levels return to normal. Your adrenaline and cortisol levels drop, your heart rate and blood pressure return to baseline levels, your breathing is slowing back down, while other systems resume their regular activities after getting the "all clear," and you're back to level zero.

But sometimes the brakes fail, and the engine keeps revving.

And when the gas is on, and we feel threatened all of the time, this creates long-term activation of the stress-response system. The overexposure to cortisol and other stress hormones that follows can disrupt almost all your body's processes. For those of you with anxiety, this is what's happening.

Are we supposed to avoid all stressful situations so that we can stay calm all the time? While a lovely thought, but that's not possible, is it? In fact, the fine folks at the Center on the Developing Child at Harvard University are quick to point out that not all stress is bad. In fact, stress is an important part of our development process because it is a natural part of life.

That's why it's important to distinguish among the different kinds of stress responses and what happens to when our brains are developing in childhood. And to be clear, these are measured by how the **stress affects the body**, not the stressful event or experience itself. What this means is that some of us can go through some really terrible experiences and actually not have a long-term negative impact from it, while other people could have experienced smaller traumas that others might perceive as not that big of a deal.

So, here's the kicker: size doesn't matter, well at least not here. Anything, and I mean *anything* that leaves a child's body in the prolonged stress state—that is the pedal is to the floor when a child doesn't know how to slow down the car racing around inside themselves—will have damaging effects on the body and the brain's architecture development. Here's how it happens.

First, there is a **positive** stress response which can be triggered by the first day in daycare without Mom nearby or getting a shot from the doctor. Having a brief increase in heart rate and mild elevations in hormone levels when experiencing this potentially uncomfortable situation for children is normal and essential to healthy development, especially if it is buffered by a comforting hug from Mom or Dad. As an adult, positive stress could be your first day at a new job or going to an event alone. If you had learned about regulation and that everything is going to be okay as a child, then those jitters go away on their own, don't they?

The next kind of stress response is called **tolerable.** This is when the body's alarm system is activated to a greater degree due to something fairly severe, like the death of a loved one, a natural disaster, or suffering a frightening injury that would involve a trip to the hospital. When children are in these elevated states of distress and they receive emotional support from the adults around them, this can help limit the period of the stress response's activation and help the brain and body recover, limiting what could be long-term damaging effects.

Finally, when a child experiences strong, frequent, or prolonged adversity without appropriate or adequate adult support to provide the buffering needed that helps the stress response calm back down, this can lead to ongoing or prolonged activation of the fight-or-flight response. And if this happens, the constant surging of hormones into the body can disrupt the development of the brain's architecture and lead to cognitive impairment, not to mention negative impacts to the immune system, cardiovascular system, and other body functions. That is what the ACES and Romanian orphanage studies uncovered.

And did you know that children can develop post-traumatic stress disorder from not receiving the proper emotional support after experiencing a traumatic event or living in an ongoing state of distress? In fact, the *Diagnostic and Statistical Manual of Mental Disorders, Fifth Edition* (DSM-V) was updated in 2013 to make it more developmentally sensitive in the wake of the new findings in neuroscience. It lowered the thresholds for younger children and found that what parents and psychologists were noting as "behavioral problems" were in fact the results of children reexperiencing trauma over and over again. It also noted that what adults viewed as traumatic experiences is not as important as understanding how the experience is viewed by the child.

Furthermore, many adults today have been diagnosed with complex PTSD, including myself, after beginning to make sense of extreme emotional responses to certain situations and relating them back to a single or series of traumatic childhood experiences in which no emotional or psychological support was provided at the time.

It was following the ACES study that the National Scientific Council on the Developing Child coined the term **toxic stress** to capture the growing and extensive scientific knowledge about the effects of the constant or prolonged activation of stress-response systems on a child's developing brain and body and how these impacts carry forward well into our adult years.

So, are you ready for another repeat? What do you think are examples of the experiences that can cause toxic stress? While some may seem obvious, others on the list defy what we thought we knew about parenting and brain development:

Physical or emotional abuse, which includes spanking or other forms of corporal punishment such as yelling or actions that incite fear in order to gain compliance, as well as applying harsh verbal abuse, teasing, shame and guilt to a child. In fact, the American Academy of Pediatrics released a policy statement in 2018 at press conference asking for the ban of all forms of corporal punishment, citing the mounting evidence that shows the long-term negative impacts on brain development and mental health.

Chronic neglect, including emotional neglect such as being told to stop crying or having feelings ignored, inappropriately dismissed, or devalued as well as not having your basic needs being consistently taken care off.

Caregiver substance abuse or poor mental health which includes, for example, alcoholism, undiagnosed depression, anxiety, or caregivers triggered and inappropriately responding to their own compounded childhood trauma.

Exposure to domestic violence or violence in the neighborhood which means watching a family member being abused or living in an environment with people being hurt regularly, because the stress response does not know the difference between a threat outside of a home or in; it only senses danger.

Family economic hardship and the ongoing burdens it creates. That is because it has been shown that living in poverty and seeing caregivers struggle with having enough resources creates stress, but also may mean parents need to work longer hours and be less available to their children.

Now, again, size doesn't matter. In the end, what research has shown is that differences between the impacts of these events and whether they are tolerable or toxic boils down to one thing: a caring and available adult for the child.

Positive and tolerable stress responses happen when there is a responsive adult available to cushion the child. Toxic stress comes from experiences that interfere with the basic brain-building activity of serve and return: a child sends out a distress signal and no one is there to answer it.

And this might be the most concerning of all the things I learned myself: emotional neglect or not having the consistent, supportive, and appropriate responses to your naturally inquisitive little mind as a child is like death by a thousand cuts. If your parents were not emotionally available to you while you were growing up, you had to sort the world out on your own.

In recent years, this understanding of the serve and return brain programming has found that emotional neglect is kind of a big deal to a developing brain. But this lack of awareness is still commonplace. In fact, we've all heard the phrase "Kids are tough! They can figure it out!" And to some extent, that is true. But unfortunately, kids aren't programmed to figure it out **well**—it's only the last resort if adults aren't around.

THE RESULTS: OUR ADULT BRAINS

One last thread before I bring this back to you and your business. Now, I could be wrong, but I'm guessing many of you probably didn't grow up in a Romanian orphanage. I want to take us back to the results from the ACE study and the dozens of research studies that followed. The key findings are ACEs are quite common, even among a middle-class population. Remember that it was found that more than two-thirds of the population report experiencing one ACE, and nearly a quarter have experienced three or more. And these adverse experiences do carry on with us throughout our lives.

I call this a tragedy we live twice: first, when we are children, forced to figure out our own emotional needs and skills. And second, when we are adults, and we are judged by the results.

Dr. Jonice Webb is a clinical psychologist and the author of *Running on Empty: Overcome Your Childhood Emotional Neglect* who noticed a lot of hallmark behaviors in her clients who seemed to come from loving and caring families but still arrived in therapy with a great deal of dissatisfaction in their lives. What she found linking these clients was an overall feeling of emptiness with no clear reasons why.

Through her work and observations, she recognized the absence of the key emotional serve and return experiences between her clients and their caregivers and the subsequent adult challenges they now faced as a result.

One of those challenges that relates directly to business and reasons why many business owners struggle with is poor self-discipline. Self-discipline again is not a skill we are born with but something we are taught and given experiences to reinforce and strengthen. However, even a caring parent can miss out on giving their child opportunities to be challenged in ways that they learn to not overindulge or to be forced to figure out how to complete what seem to be boring or mundane tasks. Without guidance or modeling of self-discipline in childhood, Dr. Webb identifies the following issues for adults that I do see pop up in the

lives of entrepreneurs and contribute heavily to their
business success:

- Feelings of being lazy
- Procrastination
- Can't meet deadlines
- Over-indulgence in eating, drinking, sleeping, and even
  spending money
- Bored with a slower-paced life
- Avoid detailed or mundane tasks
- Feeling of disappointment in yourself for not
  doing more
- Chronically an underachiever
- Feel disorganized but know that you can do better

And she is quick to point out early that no parent is perfect.
In fact, many of you reading this probably do have parents
who are fine, good people. Most parents simply struggle with
trying to do what's best for their child. And further, many
emotionally neglectful parents were emotionally neglected
themselves and probably didn't know it.

Okay, what does this all have to do with starting your
own business? Let's start by circling back on this trip and
revisit what the mounting research from neuroscience and
psychology tells us are the core capabilities adults use to
manage life and work effectively:

- Planning—Being able to make plans, carry them out, and
  set and meet goals.
- Focus—Concentrating on what's most important at any
  given time.

- Self-Regulation—Having the ability to control how we respond to our emotions and stressful situations.
- Awareness—Noticing people and situations around us and how we all fit into the picture.
- Mental Flexibility—Being able to adapt to changing situations.

And why would anyone have any difficulties with these skills? Well, again, let's review what research has to tell us.

First, serious early adversity and trauma can lead to higher levels of toxic stress responses which in turn lead to a higher risk of disrupted executive function abilities. And if that is the case, then if we are still in chaotic, threatening, or unpredictable environments that leave us feeling a bit out of control, we are going to possibly show some poor self-regulation behaviors and impulse control issues. This will look a bit like chasing after fun projects or ideas instead of working on what you know you should be doing.

We might also feel a low sense of self-efficacy or powerlessness, which is the belief that one can be an agent in improving one's life. And if you don't feel you are ultimately the architect of your own future, then it goes without saying you are missing an essential component of executing and following through on goals and goal-oriented tasks, which is one of the key functions of operating a business.

But finally, sometimes we decide we want to start our businesses because we are attracted to the idea of making more money. This desire could be the result of living in a situation where we are financially strapped or feeling the burdens of not having enough to make ends meet. But poverty can also overload our self-regulation processes because we are dealing with the constant stress associated with trying to survive with inadequate resources.

As a result, many adults who have been raised in conditions of significant stress—or who are currently undergoing acute stress—struggle to keep track of the multiple problems in their lives, analyze those problems, explore options for dealing with them, and set priorities for how best to move ahead.

Stress also hijacks our good intentions and increases the likelihood that we will be swept away by our impulses or automatic responses. So, even if we manage to develop a good business plan or to-do list of priorities, we will find it harder to stick to it if we are under a pile-up of stress.

And so, this whole chapter is now going to get boiled down to a simple math equation:

The quality of your childhood experiences = The quality of your adulting skills = The predicted quality of your business skills.

And if your adulting skills require some fine tuning (which based on the ACES research, there is a 50–66 percent chance they do, to some extent), then the probability that your venture into entrepreneurship will be fraught with problems increases. Is it strange that over half of us have some sort of exposure to adversities in childhood and over half of all businesses end up failing? And that the major reasons for business failures indicated in surveys are all related to poor executive function skills?

I suppose that could be a coincidence, but I wouldn't be writing a book if I really thought so.

GET TESTED

Now it's time for another silver lining. I want to give you a huge business and life hack that not enough people take advantage of. After breaking down how our family dynamics and childhood experiences have influenced us and shaped the programming in our heads, there is a pretty easy way to get some major insights on how all of that actually affected us that doesn't require therapy. These are called psychometric assessments or personality tests.

When we talk about **personality**, there is a widely held belief supported by a significant number of studies over a period of seventy years that there are five basic dimensions or traits that define a person's personality, known as the "Big Five." These traits have been found to be universal, and after studying people over a long period of time, they remain pretty stable. Meaning, while we all can adapt if we need to, underneath it all, we are who we are. And these traits are actually signaling how our executive function skills became developed.

The Big Five universal traits are:

Openness is the trait that features imagination, insight, and curiosity. People high in this trait are more adventuresome and creative while people low in this may struggle with abstract thinking.

Conscientiousness is the trait that features thoughtfulness, impulse control, and goal-directed behaviors. People high in this tend to plan and be organized. People low in this dislike structures and deadlines and might procrastinate on detail-oriented tasks.

Extraversion is a trait that features a drive to be sociable and even emotionally expressive. People high in this drive are outgoing and actually feel energized from being around people, while people who are low can become drained by social interactions and need recharge time after being at social events or even at a job with a lot of people.

Agreeableness is a trait that features collaboration and other prosocial behaviors. People who are high in this trait tend to show more care for other people's feeling and opinions while people low in this are less concerned and may be more competitive or at worst, manipulative.

Neuroticism is trait where some of our mental health conditions become expressed, such as depression, anxiety, and moodiness. People high in this trait experience mood swings, become easily anxious, and have trouble with emotional regulation while people low in this are stable and emotionally resilient.

Now, what I love about psychometric tests is that these assessments can show us things like:

- Whether we like detail-oriented work or not
- The way we interact and communicate with others
- If we can make decisions quickly or need time to think things through
- Whether we take charge or wait and see
- Whether we want to collaborate with others or work on our own
- If we need to be around people or if we need alone time
- How other people see us in relationships and at work

Finally, what I have seen these tests also do is not only raise our own levels of awareness of ourselves, but in return, we can begin to see that other people are complex like us. As we learn more about our inner world, we realize everyone else has one too, and there is a good chance they get tripped up on stuff like we do. I believe that personality tests not only increase our emotional intelligence but also our compassion for others and ourselves, which is a wonderful thing to have in all our relationships. In fact, if I am interested in dating anyone, I make them take one of these tests so that I have a sense of how our personalities might mesh or conflict with one another. And in case you're wondering, yes, yes, I am currently single.

How do you get access to this gold mine of information? The easiest way to begin is online, like most everything these days. If you do an internet search for "personality tests," you will get a lot of options.

In the corporate world, the three big ones are Myers-Briggs, DiSC, and Predictive Index (PI). These tests have been around for several decades and have been administered to millions of people worldwide. In fact, some of you may have had to take one at a company you worked for. These tests are not only reliable, but they have been independently studied and researched and their methods validated to be pretty accurate and useful. And there always seem to be new ones coming out as well since the demand is high.

Now, I hear people swear by one test or the other as being more insightful or accurate than others, but they are all using the same science and simply different labels. In fact, I have taken all three of the big ones and they all have told me pretty much the same thing about who I am and what I naturally prefer.

To get tested, unfortunately, DiSC and PI are typically only available through a consulting company or a company you work for. As a Certified PI Practitioner, I know that it's important that the testing, coaching, and interpretation of the results are done with an experienced and trained professional.

However, Myers-Briggs and the Enneagram both offer online versions of their tests for individuals to take, and they come with a report. Tests are around fifty dollars to do. And if you ask me, it's the best fifty dollars you can spend on your business start-up.

There are also some free versions online, but you and I both know nothing is truly free. Usually, these tests are very limited with the results and aimed to get your email address so that they can re-market other services and the real results at a price. So, instead of finding yourself on a spammer's list, I would suggest you head straight to the sources and pay. At the end of the book, I have an Appendix with a list of websites where you can find these tests.

HOW TO UNINSTALL THE PROGRAM

So, now that you realize that you could have some software running in the background that could get in the way of your best intentions, what's next? Well, I'm going to keep giving you those answers throughout the book on how to change and reprogram. But for it to work, from this point forward, I want you to do three things:

PAY ATTENTION AND BE CURIOUS

First, realize that procrastination, anxiety, poor focus, et cetera are biological responses triggered by something that has happened or is happening in your life right now. And these are physical responses you can actually feel, thanks to the hormones being flooded into your bloodstream.

Therefore, cultivating mindfulness, or the ability to become consciously aware of one's own body or situation, is a big step in the right direction.

Now, you don't need to be Buddhist monk in order to do this. All you have to do now is to see if you can start to pick up on every time your stress response is activated and then hit a pause button so that you can freeze the moment in your head and assess what is happening to you. Be curious instead of judgmental by resisting the urge to tell yourself to "quit feeling anxious" or "there's nothing to be upset about now." That is not the point. The point is to say instead to yourself, "Huh. I wonder where this feeling is coming from." Start to think of your stress responses as someone running through the halls, pulling fire alarms, and now you know that you should take your time to make sure if the building is, in fact, on fire before fleeing or grabbing a hose.

Also, next time you're sitting there, staring at the list of things you know you have to do but you can't seem to motivate yourself to complete, ask yourself, "What do I think is happening right now? Why do I want to binge watch TV at this moment instead of scheduling my social media posts?" And don't judge the reasons, just note them.

Where you want to go once you start to pick up on all the ways your body feels when it's triggered is how you think that alarm signal was programmed. You don't need to solve it or fix it right away, just start with getting into the practice of questioning it.

REMEMBER CHANGE IS POSSIBLE...

I want you to start to take stock of all of the times you are being activated and maybe figure out why because we can actually do some remodeling on our brains—without the need for a lobotomy!

Amelia explains, "For a long time, we thought that we had all the brain cells we're ever going to have. That is, if we lose one, it's not going to come back. But also, we used to think that what you have becomes totally fixed after a certain point in brain development and can't be changed. But science is showing that is really not the case."

So what Amelia is talking about is the discovery of **neuroplasticity,** which is the ability for humans to form and change the connections in our brains through the process of blooming and pruning that we learned about earlier in this chapter.

And so neuroplasticity, to me, is the bright beacon of hope in all of this because it is not limited to just simple things—once you identify other connections that you'd like to change, like your fear of speaking in public or flying, perhaps you can overcome that fear. And through hitting the pause button, figuring out what you really want to do or how to respond, and being committed to practicing your new behaviors over and over again, you will find that new connections will form and be strengthened and the old ones will weaken.

...BUT GRACE IS NECESSARY.

In the end, you now know that many of the issues that undermine our abilities to successfully perform as a businesswoman may be due to the fact that our **adult** abilities to apply adult thinking to situations are in conflict with a programmed brain based on **childhood** experiences.

And since that is the case, then we also must realize we need to give ourselves a bit of grace. How do we do that? Well, for one, it starts with knowing that some of the things you do or don't do that leave you feeling ashamed and telling yourself, "you should know better!" have a reason behind them.

When talking about how childhood trauma impacts us as adults, Amelia answers, "You know, one of the ways that I like to talk about trauma is to think about how as humans, we are born to survive and hopefully thrive in whatever environment we're born into. And some of us have experiences that are traumatic. And so, our little brain made the connections that were important for us to survive and thrive in that environment. These connections created the patterns of behavior that our brain thought we needed at that time. It's not necessarily that it is the wrong connection. It was the right connection for that time—they were what a child needed to survive a really challenging situation. But those might be the very same connections that make it more difficult to survive and thrive as an adult and then they become no longer the right connections for us."

So, be ready to cut yourself some slack. Some things in your life will change forever once you start to work on them. Others, depending on how strongly the neural connections were used and reinforced over time, will remain. But you can learn to recognize that you are experiencing a false alarm and not be lured into the needless panic that follows.

Now, are you beginning to see that adult life skills and successful business skills look eerily similar?

And are you beginning to understand that we weren't born with these skills, but that they had to be taught to us while we were kids from our interactions with adults?

And, most importantly, are you seeing that not having these skills or struggling with them is not your fault? Read that again.

If all of this is making sense, then we are really going to get some shit done together.

●●●

Chapter Four

HOW TO BE PAID WHAT YOU'RE WORTH

> *"Financial independence is paramount. My mom always says that when a woman is financially independent, she has the ability to live life on her own terms."*

–Priyanka Chopra

You know, of all the things I learned in my life, this topic we are about to tackle really pisses me off.

It started when I sat down and thought about all of the choices I consciously made for myself to help me be successful, wealthy, and independent. But when I kept seeing myself stalling out, I just felt like maybe I wasn't working hard enough or that I was cursed. I held out hope that someday it would happen.

Then, all my fantasies came crashing down when I started looking into the realm of money disorders and saw that no matter what I wanted to do, I was fucked. I was sabotaging myself in a multitude of ways and this collection of actions and beliefs was undermining everything I was doing.

See, the reality is that financial freedom is not linked to your ability to do math. Your path to your financial independence is here in this chapter. I mean this. This chapter is going to be the real key to unlocking your earnings potential—more than anything else I teach you about business. Because if we go back again to our business statistics and once again, why business owners said they failed, the number two reason was "ran out of cash." But, if we add up all of the money related reasons on the list, it was the source for 55 percent of the failures surveyed! You are about to learn the secrets behind the statistics.

First, what are the financial disadvantages women have in the world? Well, I've covered a few already, but here are some more. A 2019 report by the Institute of Women's Policy Research found that not only do women earn less than men in all occupations, women are even earning less than men in the twenty most common occupations traditionally held by women, also known as the **pink-collar** jobs like nursing, teaching, and clerical.

The "Women, Money, and Power" study commissioned by Allianz Life Insurance Company of North America found that despite advances for women in the workforce, women's confidence is declining. They noted that fewer women (38 percent) identify themselves as the breadwinner in the family than 60 percent in 2013, and that women feel like they are being left out of the financial planning decisions in their own households.

Startling, however, are the findings from the 2016 Global Financial Literacy Excellence Center's (GFLEC) study that not only is financial illiteracy widespread, it is worse among women, which is extremely problematic when census studies show that women live longer than men and need more money saved to care for their needs. In fact, the researchers also found evidence that the death of a spouse was an important fact in an older widow slipping into financial hardships.

The GFLEC study also showed large gender gaps in several countries across all marital, educational, income, and age groups and socioeconomic categories. Young, old, rich, poor, high school diploma, or graduate degree, women are less likely to answer financial literacy questions correctly and more likely to state they don't know the answers to the questions.

And the implications of this are that financial literacy is linked to other areas:

- Saving and planning for retirement
- Understanding fees when it comes to investments
- Borrowing money at lower costs
- Having resources to protect against unexpected financial shocks, like death or divorce

So, what is the solution? Well, the standard line of thinking is to give women access to this knowledge and education, and they will improve. Seems logical, right?

But do you really think the reason we are at financial disadvantages is that, as a collective group of humans, we failed to grasp the concepts of basic fourth grade math? I have an engineering degree that says otherwise.

WHY ARE WOMEN UNDEREARNERS?

So, then how did this all happen? How did women fall way behind on the gender pay gap? How did we fall for the crap interest rates on credit cards? Why aren't we saving enough money for retirement? Why don't we get to receive investments and loans to support our businesses like our male counterparts do? And most importantly: Why don't we *care?*

Well, it starts at the socially constructed set of behaviors, activities, and attributes we ascribe to what it means to be a "man" and what it means to be a "woman" which are called **gender roles.** These gender roles impacted our parents and their parent's beliefs about themselves and about you. Gender roles are propagated in culture, work, media, and the educational system.

We are bombarded regularly with messages from friends or associates on social media about what "real men" and "real women" are like and how they should act. In fact, gender roles are used as means of social control as well, punishing people who don't behave the way they are "supposed" to. This form of punishment is called a **microaggression**. And it doesn't matter that if it's changing now, the problem is we're all wired by what we were already taught, remember? And we'll talk more about microaggressions in another chapter.

Now, gender roles are hardly ever based on actual biology except for the one facet that a uterus equals children and therefore all activities related to kids belong to the

Uterus Holders. The rest, however, are based largely on religion, economics, and power. These roles then lead to **gender stereotyping**. Noted as having significant impacts to women worldwide, gender stereotyping is defined by the United Nations Commission on Human Rights as "the practice of ascribing to an individual woman or man specific attributes, characteristics, or roles by reason only of her or his membership in the social group of women or men."

Key gender-based stereotypes that we've all grown up with and which still exist today directly impact money and women's wealth are:

Personality Traits—Women are often expected to be accommodating, emotional, collaborative, helpful, and compliant while men are raised to be independent, self-confident, and aggressive.

Domestic Roles—Some people expect that women will take care of the children, cook, and clean the home, even if they are employed outside the home. On the other hand, men are expected to take care of the finances, work on the car, and do the home repairs.

Gender-Specific Occupations—People quickly assume that there are careers "more suited" for women like teachers, nurses, and secretaries, while men are better suited for leadership positions as well as careers in science, technology, or politics.

Wanting to know more, I spoke with financial psychologist and author Dr. Brad Klontz about women and money, and I asked him if he noted any other differences between how girls and boys are parented when it comes to money. And he said, unfortunately, that the gender-based stereotypes create an entire upbringing around money and women being socialized to not worry about, not pay attention to, or to even fear handling money decisions. This in turn leads to a lifetime of self-defeating behaviors and an overall lack of confidence when it comes to money in many ways.

Brad notes, "We have been giving messages to little girls that are very different from what's given to little boys about money, including messages that it's okay to be financially dependent on a male."

However, this message is detrimental because it is telling girls they are not as good with money as boys, and that, in turn, also impacts women's overall sense of entitlement or belief that they truly deserve to be paid for the work they do. Brad continues, "It can hamper a woman's ability to advocate for herself in terms of negotiations around salary. Or it impacts the subjective mindset of 'Upward mobility is available for me and actually I deserve it.'"

One study that confirmed this was published in 2012 by team of researchers from Tulane University and the University of California, Santa Barbara, who looked at gender differences in feelings of entitlement. They consistently found in their own study activities and in the results of other studies that men expected to be paid more for their work than women did.

In fact, in one exercise they did with participants, the women in the study completed more of the tasks with a higher degree of accuracy than the men. They were all asked then given a chance to provide themselves, discreetly, a bonus and to choose how much they felt it should be. Again, the men bonused themselves more than the women, even though they didn't do as much work!

But even when their inputs were equal, men still believed they were entitled to receive greater outcomes than the women believed they were entitled to receive.

Okay, so how can we identify if we are actually suffering from this inherent lack of self-confidence? How does this show up in our behaviors? Well, we are going to find out if you've been taught to be an **underearner**.

To know if you are an underearner, we have to learn another psychology term: cognitive dissonance. In her book *The Secrets of Six-Figure Women*, author Barbara Stanny points out that most women will deny they are a chronic underearner because it means they will be confronted with the fact that they will now have to do something about it. So, in order to not run into the roadblock right away, let's talk about the mental discomfort you are about to feel in this chapter.

Cognitive dissonance is the theory that helps explain why people will sometimes go to great lengths to account for thoughts, words, and behaviors that seem to contradict each other. In other words, when someone provides you with new information that challenges a deeply held belief you have about yourself and it undercuts your self-image, you are apt to deny this information is true. So, if someone says, "Hey you are personally accountable for why you are broke," you will

143

make an excuse for your actions with something like, "No, it's because my industry pays very little" or "I don't believe that money is that important" or find something else that confirms you are right and they are wrong.

But here's the cool thing: We know when we are experiencing cognitive dissonance because we feel it in our bodies. Our brains detect the new information as danger to our belief system and our nervous system gets a bit activated. Why is this danger? Well because our brains are lazy and love to automate, so they don't really want to rewrite the programs if they don't have to. They will fight the intruder of new information off and tell us, "Hey, don't listen to them. I know it's not true. Relax and don't worry, I got this."

So, when it comes to money, for example, you tell yourself that of course you don't want to be broke or that you are tired of living paycheck to paycheck. And those are probably genuinely true statements. They were for me. But the problem was that I regularly engaged in behaviors that assured I would never move beyond my current state. Because what I wanted and what I truly believed were at odds with one another.

How does this look? In my case, cognitive dissonance was believing I wanted to be wealthy and working hard to make good money and elevate myself, but when I couldn't make ends meet, it would be because the economy was bad. Or the divorce was costly. Or I had unexpected car repairs. Or spending money eating out every night was justified because I was too tired to cook and who cares, I could afford it. Or whatever really valid reason I could find and blame. Because in my head, I was too smart to be that dumb to sabotage my own financial future.

But I was.

In reality, I was undermining my own efforts by scooping away the dirt beneath my feet, one small handful at a time. I did this by not paying bills on time or buying a few extra things online that I didn't need instead of making a payment on an overdue credit card.

I also did it by constantly reminding myself and my kids, "we don't have enough money for that," words I constantly heard from my own mother growing up. While I was good at running the finances at my bigger businesses and establishing tight, workable budgets and projections, at home, I was winging it. Now that doesn't make sense, does it? If I can do money in business, then my home problems must not be my fault, right? That was my cognitive dissonance.

So, as we start to go through some of these inconsistencies between what we think we want and believe about money versus what we actually do, you are probably going to feel some shame or denial. And that's perfectly normal. But remember that feeling of discomfort means you are aware now of an opportunity for growth and change. Real growth. Real change.

Let's begin by circling back to figuring out if you are an underearner. This is going to be a great time to read slowly and note how and where each of the following statements hit you. If you feel your cognitive dissonance kick in, remember what I said earlier about being curious, not judgmental with yourself. Just try to hit the pause button on all the excuses that immediately come to your mind and become a third-person observer to them. For example, when your brain goes into protection mode with instant denial or "Yeah, but…" say to yourself, "Oh, that's interesting. I wonder where that is coming from."

Back to Barbara Stanny and her book: when she was doing her research, she culled information from more than 150 women in a variety of different professions and income levels. She noticed there were two very distinct groups of women: high-earners and chronic underearners. She also found that there were several distinct traits, behaviors, and mindsets that besieged the underearning women, no matter what field they worked in or their educational background:

- Underearners are attracted low-paying jobs because they don't think they have a choice.
- Underearners underestimate their worth and constantly undercharge.
- Underearners are willing to work for free or give away their expertise regularly.
- Underearners are terrible negotiators.
- Underearners believe money and the wealthy are corrupt.
- Underearners believe in "Mo' Money, Mo' Problems."
- Underearners are quick to blame others for their problems.
- Underearners constantly put their dreams on hold for others.
- Underearners feel guilty and "selfish" when they choose themselves.

- Underearners live in a constant state of financial chaos.
- Underearners find ways to avoid dealing with money like not looking at bills or balancing their checkbooks.

If any of those sound close, or maybe you're a little skeptical still, have you ever said things like, "I am proud of my ability to make do with very little" or "I don't need money; recognition and praise are all I need"? And if you were to look at your current finances, are you in debt, with very little, if any, savings, and don't really know where all your money is going?

High-earning businesswomen, on the other hand, will say things like, "I am confident in my ability to make money" or "I am determined to get paid what I'm worth" or "I know where every penny goes and I regularly set budgets." And if those connect more closely with you, then you are probably already operating with a high-earning mindset or at least on the way to becoming one, so that's good.

Now, when we engage or identify a chronic pattern of self-destructive financial behaviors like the ones I just listed, it means we may have a **money disorder** that has developed in our life. Funnily enough, however, the origins of these disorders may not always stem from money itself. They can be from subtle behaviors or expression of certain values, and yes, the impact of gender roles. They can also be coping mechanisms or responses to certain stressors we experience in the way one might choose to drink or take drugs. In fact, because Americans are very reluctant to talk about their money problems publicly, most of us don't realize what we are doing or why and so we don't readily equate our money problems with coping mechanisms.

In his book *Mind Over Money,* Brad lists several common money disorders that affect men and women alike. Of this list, there are several I have seen manifest specifically in business.

Compulsive Buying or the irresistible impulses to buy and continue to buy despite it causing a lot of problems. I have seen businessowners spend way more money than they earn on a variety of needless expenses and justify it despite the fact that it's clearly hurting their business.

Workaholism is a form of an addiction where one feels an intense and overwhelming inner drive to work, feels guilty or depressed when not working, and often does not enjoy work very much. Brad notes that this a family disease, often passed down through the generations through modeling and a family belief about working hard.

Financial Denial is a fallback mechanism for people who are experiencing financial stress attempting to cope by simply not thinking about money or trying to avoid dealing with it. In a study of over a thousand Americans, 36 percent admitted that they try to avoid thinking about money, making this an extremely common disorder. One way we see this is by ignoring and not paying bills on time or at all, mostly because you don't think there's enough money. This one is insidious and self-sabotaging because not paying bills increases the financial stress and the late fees increase the debt.

Financial Infidelity is another extremely common disorder, affecting about 41 percent and includes lying about, hiding, or omitting information about one's financial behaviors from one's spouse or even business partners.

How money disorders rule over us can vary, from having little to no influence or being a very strong presence. When I spoke with Brad specifically about the topic of women and the most common money disorders he's seen, he said it tends to be three major ones, which Barbara noted as well.

Undervaluing ourselves. Okay, not a big shock, especially since we touched on the lower levels of self-confidence women display with money earlier. But as Brad says, this is a major, self-destructive money disorder for women. "So basically, you're not valuing your work or you're allowing yourself to exist in a group of people who continue to not value your work, and those things are very much interrelated. And so, then you chronically undercharge and probably overdeliver! And, whatever you put a price tag on, people will agree with you. And so, underearning is a really powerful one that can be extremely devastating."

Being too nice. Groomed to be collaborative means we put ourselves second for the greater good. "The other thing is that women have a tendency to be pretty nice. And there's a lot of research to support this too. Women are much more agreeable. They're much more focused on loving the people around them and being concerned with their needs." As Brad notes, this then comes out in women's tendencies to do a very poor job at negotiating salaries, not raising fees, or basically caving in when their request for a raise is turned down.

Financial enabling. Brad calls financial enabling "the financial help that hurts" because it's coming from a place of caring on the part of the woman wanting to help, but she may be actually supporting another person whose need for money is because that person is misbehaving with their own money. Sadly, this need to help can spring from feelings of guilt and can make women who earn more than their close friends and family especially vulnerable. "That sense of guilt and that sense of disconnection from your family and friends can be a huge psychological trigger for you to give away your money," Brad cautions.

Research is confirming and experts agree that the true key to success with money, whether it is increasing your personal savings or making a profit with your business, ultimately lies in psychology and not in economics.

So, before we go further, I really needed to make sure you could see some potential blocks you might have. Because the next exercise won't be as useful if you are carrying underlying, underearning ideas.

EXERCISE

Ask yourself the following and write down your answers. Remember, no judgment. Just curiosity.

1. Do you think you're an underearner? If so, what underearning behaviors do you currently have?

2. Do you think you have any of the money disorders mentioned? Which ones and where do you think they come from?

3. How was money handled in your family? What messages were you given about work and money? What was your mother like with money? Your father? Was there emotional trauma with money?

4. What was your biggest fear about money when you were younger? Your parents' fears? What's your greatest fear now?

HOW MUCH DO YOU WANT OR NEED TO MAKE?

Before I keep taking you on this journey of how our minds, money, and businesses all mix together, we're going to stop for a minute. I want you to now figure out your personal financial goals that you want this business to help you achieve. This part is more important than you think because if you don't set real money targets, you are doomed to underearn. I'm going to show you how that happens.

In the second chapter, I wanted you to dip your toe into the water and force the issue of thinking about your salary. But now we're going to think bigger and have you set some real goals to use in the following examples.

To do this, I want you to think of your financial goals as four levels of a video game. Level One is where you begin, and Level Four means you beat the game. Now, unlike a video game, these are not fantasies but real targets for you. Take time to figure these four levels out and write them down.

Level One: What do I need to make to be financially secure? This is the amount of money that you have to make in order to have your basic needs met and peace of mind. In other words, this is the lowest amount you need to earn. For this exercise, resist the urge to include your partner's salary in here, if you have one. I want you to approach this as if this business you are going to work hard on and invest in is going to be able to take care of you completely if you need it to. To do this step, then, make sure you sit down with your household numbers and know what all of your monthly and yearly expenses are so that you can get an accurate picture.

Level Two: What do I want to make to be able to upgrade my life? This is the income level that covers all of your expenses and gives you the extra to upgrade your lifestyle. Now, at this level, you will have to define what "upgrades" are to you. It could be money for more exotic vacations, moving into a bigger house, buying a nicer car, or having a slush fund for luxuries. Make that list and add it to your expenses and see what you end up with.

Level Three: At what point am I making enough money to be financially separate from working at all? This level means you are creating enough passive or residual income with your business that you don't need to be involved on a day-to-day basis. In other words, this means you don't have to work, and all of your expenses are paid for. Think of it as an early retirement. Now, to achieve this level faster, you might define your expenses as those you pulled together for your Level One income and give up on the upgrades, that's up to you.

Level Four: How much money gives me financial power? This is the mega level—the final level of the game—how much money does it take for your business to earn so that you don't have to work, and you can have everything you ever dreamed of.

The point here is to get you to start to think less about your income as a traditional salary and see it as the path to the destination you are heading toward. One of the biggest appeals of entrepreneurship, again, is freedom. And if you stop worrying about how much other people are making and comparing yourself to them, you begin to break free of a few traps that can keep you underearning. Therefore, these levels are the numbers we want to use in the next sections because they mean something to you and your freedom. And this small shift in mindset will give you huge results, so don't take this lightly.

BASIC BUSINESS FINANCIALS

First, there are only two things you have to know that will have the most profound impacts on the financial state of a small or micro business. If your business is not making money:

1. The price is too low
2. The expenses are too high, or
3. Both are true

Yes, I know, sales matter too, but not if the price is too low or the expenses are out of control. In fact, a common business mistake is to focus on bringing in more sales, while ignoring the fact that the business isn't really making money because, again, they aren't charging enough to begin with, or they are wasting money. I'm going to prove it in a minute.

To do that, I'm going to do some math and walk you through some examples that will show you how self-defeating money behaviors play out in the numbers. If there is one reason I love numbers so much, it's because the numbers don't lie.

But before I do that, I must make sure we are all working from the same basic level of business financial literacy.

First, it costs money to run your business. These costs are called your operational expenses. Now, operational expenses come in two flavors: fixed and variable. Also sometimes referred to as **overhead** costs, **fixed expenses** are the things that you pay on a regular timeframe, whether you are making a bunch of money or not.

Typical overhead expenses are:

- Ongoing rent or mortgage on an office or store
- Insurance
- Utilities like your phone, electricity, internet
- Administrative costs like a weekly bookkeeper, office supplies, your accountant once a year

- Marketing and advertising like networking group memberships, social media ads
- Monthly software or online subscriptions
- Employee salaries/payroll

Now the next category of costs are the **variable expenses.** These are also called the "cost of sales" (COS) or the "cost of goods" (COG) and they are the things you buy or pay for **only when** you have a service to provide or an order to fill. So, naturally, if you have no sales, you have no need to buy jewelry making supplies, right? But if you have an order, you may need to buy things to fill that order. This is why they are called "variable" because they go up and down. Examples of cost of sales/goods are:

- Raw materials for goods/products
- Tools and supplies for making your goods/products
- Shipping supplies
- Travel to visit coaching clients

This is a good time to highlight another common mistake. For someone in the maker businesses, when you are calculating your COS, I want you to remember that many of your materials and supplies are purchased in bulk, not one part at a time. Also, there is waste or spoilage that needs to be accounted for that a lot of first-time business owners fail to account for in their numbers.

But what also happens more often than not is that you buy a lot of extra stuff that you need to make something but doesn't end up being a physical part of the finished product, so it gets forgotten. These are called **consumables** and include things like the fuel for your torches, sandpaper, personal protection equipment like latex gloves and masks, boxes for shipping, etc. They are a very real part of the COS. However, when you accidentally leave them out of the calculations, you can really mess up your numbers. For one, it gives you an inaccurate COS of your products, but also, people are surprised by how much they overspend on consumables because it's never linked in their heads to the impact on the prices they are changing.

So, if you have bulk silver wire and doing the math tells you that you can make five rings from one foot of it and it cost you $10 per foot, you may be apt to quickly say that the COS is $2 per ring for the silver. But, if you were to look at what you made from that one foot of wire and it was on average only three rings due to waste, mistakes or sizing differences, then the COS for silver was $3.33, a difference of nearly 50 percent.

Taking this a step further and realizing that you have to actually look at the total costs of everything over the past year and divide by the number of pieces you actually made that were available to sell (**finished inventory**), you will get the real COS.

This means, for example, if you spent $2,000 in all your ring-making supplies and raw materials last year and had a finished inventory of a hundred rings (sold and unsold), then your cost of sales was $20 per ring, not $3.33. That's a difference of 143 percent!

Now, most people start their business and enter with the mindset that profit is what is leftover to pay themselves with. To be honest, this is the exact line of thinking that can make businesswomen chronically underpaid or trapped in their business and unable to expand because it is perpetuating the belief that you come last, which is not true—in life or in business. That's why we have to talk about what profit really is for a business.

A simple definition of **profit** is that it is the amount of money left over after you add up all of your sales and subtract from it all of your expenses, **which includes your salary**. Profit has two flavors, however, based on the two buckets of expenses. First, when you make a sale and subtract the variable costs (COS), whatever is left is **gross profit**. But you're not done yet. This is why you have to have your overhead costs broken out separately. Your gross profit is called your **contribution**, and it's what is used to pay your fixed expenses.

So, from your gross profit, you have to subtract out all of the overhead expenses and then what you finally have left is your **net profit**.

Now, I have coached many small business owners who track all of their expenses in one big lump which is a mistake. For one, you want to structure your business to have as low of an overhead as possible so that you can maximize your take-home or net profits. That means you want to know the difference between a cost a customer is going to pay for (COS) and a cost that comes out of your gross profits from that sale (overhead).

When a company has profit, they can choose to do a few things with it. In some cases, yes, the extra money is paid to the owners or shareholders. In corporate lingo, this is sometimes called a dividend. In your case, if you are a solopreneur, you could treat your profits or a portion of them as a bonus to you on top of what you're earning, called a **draw** or distribution.

However, businesses also decide to **retain** their profits so that they can be saved and used to either expand the business, upgrade equipment, or hire employees in the future. If, for example, you include in your pricing a percentage that is earmarked specifically for a new future employee, then it is giving you the exit path to turn over the work to another when you are ready to grow or leave the business. If you don't work that in sooner than later, it could be a bit like chipping out a doorway into a concrete wall—very hard to do.

Having a business that earns a profit is also beneficial in the event you want to borrow money to grow, either from a bank or private investor. Your ability to be smart and continually earn profits shows that you are savvy and that your business is a low risk for default on a loan. So, when you are ready to expand and move from your home to an office or get financing to buy a delivery vehicle, showing profit will be critical. And, by the way—if you don't have a line item for your salary, bankers and investors may be skeptical of your numbers.

How do you know what to add for profit? That's a great question that I'm about to give you a lousy answer to: it depends. To figure out how much profit you want, you must first know what you are saving for and what that costs. Or, if you don't know, think of it in the same way as you do your personal savings goals. A rule of thumb that goes back to the classic book *The Richest Man in Babylon* by George S. Clason is to save one out of every ten dollars you earn. So, if you want to keep it easy, you have my permission to start there but personally, I'm more aggressive and always like starting at 30 percent.

Now, your profits could be much higher in certain industries because the market is charging way more for goods and services than it takes to make or provide them, and you might find that you can actually realize a profit of 100 percent. So, another way to decide how much profit you want to add is do some internet research and see if you can find what standard profit margins are in the industry you are working in.

However, the bare minimum any business needs to meet is the **break-even point**. This is the lowest threshold of sales that brings in enough revenue to pay all the expenses, without profit. And figuring this out is tricky because it's a bit of a game between adjusting the pricing of your products or services or adjusting how much you sell. It can be looked at as figuring out how to balance scales, through a bit of experimentation as you put in or take away weights in each pan.

So, if you don't know what you're going to charge right away, then to calculate it, you must have an idea of what you think you can produce and sell in a year. This is your **sales target**. Now, I know that feels a bit like putting the cart before the horse because you want to say, "I have no idea how much I'm going to sell," but the fact is businesswomen develop projections and goals; hobby owners do not. And to do this, you need to remember to not make that other common mistake: assuming you are 100 percent efficient. I already told you that you're not.

In the beginning, you probably need to expect that half of your time will be making your products or providing your services and half of your time will be with the office and support work required to support the business, such as paying bills, posting on social media, marketing, ordering materials, and completing the paperwork to fill orders or invoice your clients.

This brings us to another common mistake I see businessowners do: adding up only the hours or minutes you spend working on the finished item, or the **value-added or billable work**, and forgetting the other work involved, like restocking shelves, setting up your tools, packing up the orders, cleaning paint brushes, driving to meetings, or the **non-value-added** work. So again, instead of trying to look at just one piece or one hour of consulting or coaching, step back and see how many total pieces or hours on average you do in a week's time and how much was billable and how much wasn't.

If after you run your business awhile, you develop a more accurate number, great. But if you are starting out and need to know where to begin, I've given you a stake in the ground to aim for.

DETERMINING YOUR VALUE

Okay, we're here. Stretch your legs and get ready. Armed with basic business financial literacy and your personal income goals, let's start to run some fun examples and see how money disorders worm their way into how we price our goods and services.

So, let's look at the two main ways a selling price is determined for any product or service. First, **cost-plus** is the traditional method of setting a price by taking all your expenses and adding a desired profit margin to them. The **price-minus** method, on the other hand, is taking a price that is already established in the market or the goal you want your product or service to be sold out and then working backward to see what your expenses, sales targets and break-even points need to be. Deciding which approach to take depends on a few things, but the most important one is what you learn by doing some **market research**.

In other words, you see what other businesses are charging for similar products and services to yours, making sure to get a wide variety so that you can see who is on the low end and who is on the high end, and why. Now, I have done a little of that for these examples I'm going to show you, so let's begin.

COST-PLUS EXAMPLE FOR A MAKER

Let's say you are a jewelry maker with a home-based workshop. At your current pace you've been working, you can produce three pieces of jewelry per week as well as spend two days doing office, design, and sales work. Your overhead expenses include paying for the internet, a cell phone, a program to make cool social media graphics of your work, and your annual website renewal fees. Also, you've budgeted an extra $100 per month to spend on advertising and other marketing expenses for a total of $300 per month.

Based on your personal budget, you figured that you needed a salary of $65,000 per year to cover all of your household and living expenses, giving you Level One financial peace of mind. So, your businesses total fixed overhead expenses in a year are:

Total Annual Overhead Expenses =

$$\$3,600 + 65,000 \text{ salary}$$
$$= \$68,600$$

Now, to make the three pieces per week over the course of one year, it will cost you about $45 per piece in silver, gemstones, and other miscellaneous supplies. Since you want to also have time off, you figure that in one year you will be able to produce 150 pieces total (three pieces per week for 50 weeks).

Cost Per Unit to Cover Overhead Only:

$$\$68,600/150$$

$$= \$457.33$$

Cost Per Unit in Variable Expenses: $45

Total Cost Per Unit to Breakeven: $502.33

Okay before we go any further, are there any of the crafters/makers reading this book doing a jaw-dropping "What the fu...!?"

Do you see what I see? Yeah. Some of you just got a glass of cold water tossed in your face and a wake-up call telling you you're likely either not charging enough or you're not making enough stuff to ever turn your side hustle hobby into a viable, self-sustaining business at the pace you're going right now. How do I know this? Because I've seen what makers usually charge for their works. They charge what they think people would pay for the pieces if they bought them, not what it actually costs to make them.

But don't worry—I'm not here to scold you or shame you. You're not alone. Remember what all the research and experts have said: Most women are not charging enough. So, we'll come back to our jewelry maker later because I love her and want her to be successful and we'll keep tackling this.

COST-PLUS EXAMPLE FOR A SERVICE PROVIDER

Let's say you are a personal coach or consultant and just like our jewelry maker, you are able to work out of your own home, saving you the overhead costs associated with renting an office. And again, like the jewelry maker, you have similar fixed overhead expenses, but you are also a member of a few networking referral groups that meet monthly, so your fixed overhead is closer to $500 per month.

You are looking for a career that offers you Level Two lifestyle upgrades. You know you only need $65,000 to meet all of your household expenses, but you want extra money for the finer things in life, as well as to travel a few times per year and maybe upgrade to a high-rise apartment downtown. Therefore, you are looking to pay yourself $125,000 per year.

Total Annual Overhead Expenses = $6,000 + $125,000 salary
= $131,000

Now, you know that you don't actually have forty hours per week available to coach clients because you need to also spend time doing marketing work like publishing to social media, prospecting for new clients, publishing blog articles, and producing training materials for speaking engagements you do at networking events. So, you have calculated that you have only an average of twenty-five hours per week for actual billable time. And since you want to travel a couple of weeks per year, the total hours available for coaching in one entire year is 1,250 hours. Fortunately, since you use web-based conferencing, and can coach from your home, you don't have any additional variable or Cost of Sales expenses.

Cost Per Unit to Cover Overhead Only:

$$\$131,000/1,250$$
$$= \$104.80$$

Cost Per Unit in Variable Expenses: $0

Total Cost Per Unit to Breakeven: $104.80

Since you are already looking ahead and would like to expand business someday because you're gunning for getting to Level Three in the next couple of years, you want to have some extra money available for upgrading equipment for future products like video classes and online teaching. So, you're adding a profit margin of 30 percent onto your cost to determine what the selling price should be for one hour of coaching.

Cost-Plus Selling Price:

$$\$104.80 \times 1.30$$
$$= \$136.24$$

Now here is something interesting about our second example: our coach did her market research and found that the average coaching rate for her specialty niche market was $150 per hour. So, should she charge only $136 per hour for coaching or $150? Well, here's my favorite answer: that depends.

She might choose to stick to $136 because she feels it offers her a competitive advantage over the coaches who are charging $150 and it will help her keep her schedule full of clients. That could also reduce the time she has to spend on sales and recruiting new clients and it could free more hours for more coaching or she might use it for personal time. That's up to her, but let's look at an alternative.

PRICE-MINUS EXAMPLE FOR A SERVICE PROVIDER

Let's suppose our coach decides to match the market because she is entitled to be paid the same as everyone else. Now she's applying the **price-minus** strategy for determining her selling price and sales targets, and the math looks like this:

Selling Price per Unit (Hour)	$150
Variable Expenses Per Hour	$0
Contribution Toward Fixed Expenses (Price-Minus Variable)	$150

Total Annual Fixed Expenses Per Hour (Overhead + Profit):

$131,000x1.3
$170,300

Total Hours Needed to Coach	($170,300/$150)
	1,135

So, by raising her rates to match the market, she only needs to work 1,135 hours per year to make the same amount of money as charging less. Now, at first glance, the difference between 1,250 and 1,135 doesn't seem like much until you realize that it's 115 hours or almost three extra weeks!

That is either three more weeks of vacation or, if she works only twenty-five hours per week again, it's another $11,250 in revenue. Pretty amazing from just a slight bump in pricing, isn't it?

Okay, so now I want to use this same method with our jewelry maker because I think it's going to illustrate how so many women start hobby businesses and never quite figure out how to turn them from side hustles into businesses that provide a living wage. And by the way, the market number I use in my examples I found online so that I could make these as realistic as possible and something you all are welcome to verify.

PRICE-MINUS EXAMPLE FOR A MAKER

We have our jewelry maker who specializes in hand-hammered, cuff style, adjustable rings and bracelets made from steel. During her market research, it was found that there are lots of custom, handmade ring makers and some even do similar designs. After reviewing several different designers, it looks like the average price is $25 per ring. Using that price as a standard and knowing that the COS for each of her rings is $10 for the steel bands, packaging and cost to ship, she set out to see what her break-even point is for her business if she wanted to earn $65,000 per year and cover her overhead expenses of $3,600 per year.

167

Selling Price per Unit (Ring) $25

Variable Expenses Per Ring $10

Contribution Toward Fixed Expenses (Price-Minus Variable)

$15

Total Annual Fixed Expenses Per Hour (Overhead + Salary):

$65,000 + $3,600
$68,600

Total Rings to Sell to Breakeven

($68,600/$15)
4,573

I'm going to take a sip of my margarita and give you a minute to catch your breath.

Ready? Yes, you read that number right. No, it's not a math error. She must find thirteen customers and make thirteen rings per day, every day, to break even and have a business job that pays her enough to live her Level One lifestyle.

Okay, so maybe some of you out there are yelling at the book, *"The COS for the rings are actually $2 each. This calculation is unfair!"*

Uh huh. I'll bite. Let's go.

Selling Price per Unit (Ring) $25

Variable Expenses Per Ring $2

Contribution Toward Fixed Expenses (Price-Minus Variable)

$23

Total Annual Fixed Expenses Per Hour (Overhead + Salary):

$65,000 + $3,600

$68,600

Total Rings to Sell to Breakeven

($68,600/$23)

2,982

Oh good. It dropped. Now she only has to sell eight handmade rings per day every day to break even. So glad we fixed that. Yes, I'm being sarcastic. No, I'm not being cruel. I promise.

So, bear with me as I keep pushing buttons. Now, because most of our hobby owners aren't cranking out a couple of thousand pieces a year, let's look at the price-setting scenario that really happens instead.

THE SIDE HUSTLER PRICING METHOD

After years and years of making jewelry as a hobby and people encouraging her to sell her stuff, our gifted jewelry maker decides to turn her passion into a full-fledged business. Once she gets everything set up, she has an annual overhead of $3,600. She loves what she does because it's a creative outlet for her, so she regularly purchases supplies every month to design, make, and sell a few rings. This is another $200 per month in COS costs or $2,400 per year. She sets her price for rings at $25, because that's what everyone else is charging for the same thing. Thanks to using an online store and doing a few pop-ups at farmers markets and gift shows, she manages to sell an average of three rings per week for a total of 150 for the year.

She figures whatever money is left over (profit) will be what she earns.

Total Gross Sales	(150 x $25) $3,750
Total Expenses (Fixed & Variable)	$6000
She Paid Herself	-$2,250

Okay, are you seeing the problem?

Now, you will argue with me and say that she can pick up the pace and just make more to sell.

But you do know that if she doubles, triples, or even quadruples her output to 600 rings per year, the max she's earning in gross sales is only $15,000.

Now, subtract from that $15,000 her expenses, which are now $13,200 because the **variable expenses increase with sales**, she walked away with $1,800 in her pocket and stress from making two rings per day while also trying to find time to find an average of two new customers per day, handle the orders, the shipping, packaging, order more materials, etc.

I hear you still arguing, so yes, I know the variable expenses are pretty educated guesses on my part, but jeez, what if they were zero? First, you know they aren't, but I'll humor you and your cognitive dissonance—do you want to work that hard for only $15,000 per year? Fuck. No. Because even if it only took her twenty hours a week to produce and sell 600 rings per year, that's a pre-tax salary of $14 per hour. If it is taking up more than that, she quickly drops to minimum wage or lower. And finding the equivalent of three to six hundred customers is not easy all on its own!

"Okay, okay, how about we quadruple the ring prices?" you ask me.

And increase production because otherwise it's the same number?

"Yeah, and increase production."

Okay.

Total Gross Sales (600 x $100 per ring)

$60,000

Total Expenses (Fixed & Variable) $13,200

She Paid Herself $46,800

Okay, good job. That's better. Not great, but now you have to create a business model that sells 600 rings for $100 each (that don't cost you more than $20 to make). Totally doable, but probably not what the jewelry maker thought she was originally getting herself into.

Now we could play this numbers game all day, but hopefully you're seeing on your own the levers to pull on. For example, if you keep creeping up that selling price number, you'll see that it's really the key here. Because doubling that again to $200 pushes her to $120,000 in annual sales but keeps the total expenses the same. And now, our jewelry maker is paying herself over $100,000 per year. Then, if she takes this a little further, if she can make her expenses more efficient, that's even more money for her.

I see the gears turning now in your head as you ask me, *"But what about the market analysis that said all of the rings sell for $25?"*

Yeah, let's talk about that. Who is setting the price again? Wanna bet that those numbers are from underearners who don't really know if they are making money or not? Can we actually afford to trust those numbers we found online or at the pop-up show or do we need to find some businesses who are charging way more for their goods and services? Because I think our data is now suspect.

Now here's a trick question: do you remember the part in the second chapter where I doubled back and reminded you to use the median hourly rate for men as your rate in your financial plan? Well, I was hoping to illustrate the point that women tend to perpetuate the salary and earnings gap because they only get reference points on what they should be doing or making from **other women**. That means if you question ten women about what they should charge for their products or services, you're statistically likely to get ten answers lower than if you asked the same question to ten men!

The research team of the Tulane-UC Santa Barbara study noted the same thing. When they studied the gender differences in entitlement, they also noted that expectations or beliefs about what woman will be paid are largely influenced by social comparisons. And, because there is a gender gap in pay, then as we continue to seek same-sex social comparisons, we keep the wage gap intact! Is your mind blown right now? It should be.

So, depending on the industry you are in, you might have to question some of the market research numbers you dug up because they might be lies. Why? Because, sadly, this level of business strategy we just stepped through is not what is practiced regularly, which is why I'm covering it in such a direct, albeit sarcastic, way. And don't think this is just a woman thing. No, it's commonplace across the board. Again, remember the number two reason all businesses fail, men-owned and women-owned: "Ran out of cash" combined with "pricing or cost issues."

In fact, when I got into the wedding venue business, I had to tell two experienced businesspeople that they were losing $700 per event and leaving another $1,000 per event on the table due to underpricing themselves because they didn't do these exercises either. So, join the club.

That's why I'm here to tell you, Sister—if it's costing you money day in and day out, it's not a business. It is a hobby—no matter what industry you are in—and you're way ahead of the game if you keep it that way. In fact, keeping it a hobby can actually save you $3,600 a year in "business overhead" if you are like our jewelry maker. This is how I talk some women out of entrepreneurship completely—it isn't for everyone. And I don't want to see you being fooled by the system that is rigged against you.

Now, when I run numbers like this, I tend to get fired up and I can't call this book *The Fearless Woman's Guide to Starting a Business* if I'm not willing to call out the bullshit when I see it. But there is this emerging industry in crafting and creative entrepreneurship that is just another "pink ghetto" career. It ties up a woman's creativity, efforts, and money but does nothing to pump real dollars into her purse and allow her to have basic financial security, let alone any financial independence.

According to Etsy's own research, this maker/hobby economy is a **five billion dollar** a year industry that thrives on you, my makers reading this, as a *customer*. Yes. As a customer who places a high value on working independently, doing something you love, no matter the cost, and hoping that maybe you can offset your hobby spending with a few extra bucks.

See, you buy the materials from countless suppliers and add your endless creativity, inspiration, and **value** to the raw goods, and then occasionally sell it off to someone else. The suppliers make money from **you** whether you successfully sell your stuff or not. The online stores or platforms take their percentage off **your** sales income at each transaction. The customers get a great deal because you undercharged and you, Sister, are in the middle of it all getting screwed.

So, I'm going to call this what this is: it's not just a pink ghetto. It's a fucking **pink sweatshop** all prettied up with Instagram-worthy photos and mission statements about empowering women entrepreneurs and supporting micro businesses.

There. I said it. And you can fight me on this, but I'm going to back it up with what I keep saying in this chapter: The numbers don't fucking lie.

You look a little defeated as you stare into your glass, *"Yeah but it's been giving me extra spending money to help with bills or to buy things."*

Is it? I mean, is it really giving you "extra" money? Not to sound skeptical, but I'm skeptical. Because in my experience, many business owners from coaches to photographers have not sat down and gotten detailed with tracking their expenses to really know for sure. And you and I just ran some pretty basic numbers here.

So, when I hear that the business is someone's "side hustle" and it's some extra money to pay for their crafting habit or to buy something for themselves, I'm guessing that what they are really doing is playing the hobby owner shell-game of robbing Patricia to pay Penny. Or, more accurately, robbing themselves to pay everyone else!

Because again, the numbers don't lie, and neither does the research: Women are selling themselves short across all industries. So, whether you want to hear it or not, the reality is that the Side Hustler is not charging enough and when they make a sale, they have money *at that moment,* and it feels like "profit."

If they sat down and totaled everything up, **including the value of their labor which they almost always count as worth nothing thanks to their low sense of entitlement**, they aren't making very much, if anything at all.

The fact is, you might find that you would truly have extra money if you spent the hours you do on your craft/hobby and actually took a part-time job somewhere. You'd actually be making substantially more, but you didn't because you might have thought the job was too low paying or beneath your skills. And then guess, what? You ended up doing yourself no favors by working for the stingiest boss ever (you)!

To all of you who bought this book because you wanted to turn your side hustle into a business, I'm not saying "quit." I'm saying that if you're going to do this, be a fucking mogul about it!

At this point, looking at the faces staring back at me, I see that everyone is holding their breath a little. So, I know I need to keep going and get to the point I want you to really hear:

A lot of you have been groomed to not look at the numbers, grew up afraid of the numbers, or were taught that to look at the numbers meant you were greedy. To quote a famous movie line directed toward our heroine Dorothy, we've all been told, "Pay no attention to that man behind the curtain!" Why? Because that man has all the money!

And worse, because women have been undervaluing themselves for so long, we have collectively set the low expectation for what our services are worth. So, as we try to raise the bar and charge more, we are going to have to fight against our own herd telling us it can't be done.

Now you understand why Brad used the words "extremely devastating" to describe the problem with undervaluing or under charging for women. Because it is. But you can change that.

STRATEGIES FOR CHANGING YOUR MONEY MINDSETS

It's not easy to overcome self-destructive money behaviors or even just the uneasiness we may have with believing we are worthy and capable of asking to be paid a fair wage for what we do. I know this from my own experience. But there are simple yet major things you can do today to get you on a great start.

Find a New Herd: Whether we think that there isn't enough money, that we don't deserve it, that money is evil, or that bad things happen when we get it, one of the biggest keys to overcoming our negative beliefs about money is to start looking for evidence that proves none of these things are true. The first way to find new evidence is to do what Brad suggests and hang with different people!

"We tend to hang out with people who share similar beliefs around what's normal in terms of how much money we're making and that kind of thing. And unfortunately, if you're going to try to rise above that level or do something different like charging more for your work than what they think is normal, you're going to get tons of blowback from everyone else around you. Meanwhile, there's a whole other socioeconomic herd over here where it's just a given that, 'Of course, we're going to pay you for that asset. I mean, what world do you live in where I wouldn't pay you for that asset? That's a ridiculous idea.' And so those are the people you want to get to know and spend more time with because they really do exist."

Always Come Back to Your Big Reason Why. The research and practical experience from the professionals in the field of financial planning all agree that people who focus on their goals and plans, in relation to the lifestyle they want to be living, all do better at sticking to their plans.

This goes back to why, again, just teaching a person how to understand compounding interest isn't going to suddenly turn them into savvy money-handlers. In fact, Brad did his own study with people in five different states and found the exact same thing.

In his study, they had two groups of participants. One group was put into a financial literacy class and taught the skills of saving money and setting budgets. Another group was told instead to visualize and get excited about what they were saving for and what the benefits were to them, like a vacation or new home. Then, this group created vision boards and weren't given any financial literacy training at all.

The savings rate of the financial literacy group grew by 20 percent, which is great. But the group that got excited about their big reason "why" saw that by not saving, they were delaying the futures they really wanted for themselves and their family. This group increased their savings rates by over 70 percent!

This concept was also noted by Barbara while researching her book. In fact, she found that women reported that once they shifted away from just focusing on how much money they made and more toward a goal of living their best lives, many women started to make more money. That's why figuring out your levels is incredibly important.

Think Like a High-Earning Business Mogul. I feel like I need to end this chapter by coming back to the illustrations I provided and make sure I say this again: I am not saying that all craft or maker businesses are dead enders. That was not the point. The point was, again, to show you how they can be if you don't treat them like a business and have a business mindset. The truth is that you can become a high-earning businesswoman in any field, including the low-paying pink-collar fields—just look at men doing it already! But, seriously, it won't happen by accident. It happens with effort.

Here are the key take-aways that Barbara Stanny found in her interviews with high-earning women. They:

- Know that financial success is possible in any field.
- Don't work hard, they work smart.

- Focus on fulfilling their lifestyle goals.
- Feel the fear of rejection and cognitive dissonance, have doubts they are doing the right thing, and go for it anyway!
- Feel entitled, expect to be paid for their work, and want to make money.
- Build a nurturing group around them that will cheer them on.
- Live in a world where paying women what they are truly worth is a given.

This can be you too.

HOW I CHANGED MY MONEY MINDSETS

Thanks to taboos regarding talking about money, you don't see a lot of people admit that they are struggling. Plus, as I mentioned earlier, the discomfort we feel at the thought that we could be sabotaging ourselves makes us feel ashamed. And I will tell you, overcoming money disorders has been one of the hardest things I've ever tackled in my own journey. So, I'm going to end this chapter by laying out for you how I was hurting myself and the little things I did to stop because I want you to know that you are not alone. I want you to know it is hard work, but we are all worth it. Not only that, but as a mother, my kids deserved to see and have better so that they wouldn't be trapped themselves.

As I started this chapter, I told you that money disorders were the secret saboteurs in my own life. I generally had no issues with making money; I had problems keeping it. For years, I tried positive affirmations, meditations, manifestations, and a whole lot of other stuff from Tony Robbins to Mel Robbins! But it wasn't really until I understood what my money disorders were and where they came from that I was able to understand what they were doing to me.

I was a chronic underearner who was guilty of undervaluing myself. I was a workaholic. And I was the Queen of Financial Denial who got sick to my stomach when bills arrived because I was 100 percent certain there wasn't enough money to pay them. I had zero savings and thousands of dollars in high-interest debt. I soothed myself and my stress by spending more than I earned and felt guilty about it.

Hoping that life would dramatically change once I stopped lying to myself and admitted I was doing all of those things, I was surprised when life didn't change. I mean, after all, I set up monthly budgets again, did a cash flow analysis to examine my spending, talked with my kids about being responsible with their allowances, and on and on. But I still ignored the bills when they came in because I got the instant tingle in my chest from the worry that I couldn't pay it right now. And then when I got hit with a late fee, I was super pissed at myself because that just cost me more money that I didn't have.

And just when I figured it couldn't get any worse, I was hit with bad news that the divorce settlement I was hoping would save me from my financial woes was looking like it was further and further away. After crying in anger and frustration, I decided to take a different perspective instead. So, I grabbed a notebook, sat on the couch, and asked myself what I thought this experience was trying to teach me. And that's when I got honest with myself and realized I was still putting off addressing my actual problems and hoping to win the lottery instead.

That's when I stepped back and reviewed all the ways I had tried but couldn't follow through on my way to become more disciplined with my spending and budgeting habits. And I could see that for myself, a one-month budget was too long and too big. It gave me too much time to "soothe" myself with unnecessary purchases, especially as I was dealing with the overwhelming stress and costs of divorce.

So, I thought about my own situation like I was coaching myself and said, "Ameé, maybe one month is too much right now to handle psychologically. Instead of trying to do a hundred push-ups today, let's just start with ten."

To do that, I broke my budget down to one pay period at a time. Two weeks. I went through past bank statements and logged every expense in a spreadsheet and when I paid it and if it didn't fall into my current two-week window, I didn't worry about it. And I included everything, from the music subscription monthly fees to replenishing toothpaste and shampoo. I found it was the little things I easily overlooked that were catching me off guard. There is nothing worse than having a $25 overdraft fee due to a $9.99 charge for my movie streaming service I failed to plan for when I bought that new knife set on Amazon.

I ate the big elephant two weeks at a time. And I did it over and over again. Just two weeks at a time.

Then a funny thing happened: I went from stressing about money to realizing how much there really was. That gave me a chance to map out how to spend the resources I didn't know I had and how I could pay off debts faster. And then, after a couple of months, I noticed that if I didn't do my budget on pay day, it made me nervous. I went from being afraid of doing the budget to now being afraid of **not** doing the budget because I saw how backsliding would push me away from my dreams. I had finally successfully reprogrammed my brain in a big way.

The point of all of this is that how to shift your mindset is not a one-size-fits-all approach. It takes trial and error, and you have to be aware of what's working or not. For me, being a lover of numbers, spreadsheets, and trend analysis, it didn't make sense that I couldn't keep up with a monthly program. Instead of changing it, I just kept feeling ashamed of myself. But I also didn't give up on myself or the vision I had of a woman who was self-sufficient, financially healthy, and a positive role model for her kids so that they weren't doomed to repeat the sins of their mother.

So, as you sit down to figure out what will work for you, keep in mind that you deserve success. You deserve to be valued. And you have the abilities, right at your fingertips, to do it all.

• • •

Chapter Five

BECOMING AUTHENTIC: WHO YOU ARE & WHAT YOU STAND FOR

"If you think dealing with issues like worthiness and authenticity and vulnerability are not worthwhile because there are more pressing issues, like the bottom line or attendance or standardized test scores, you are sadly, sadly mistaken. It underpins everything."

—*Brené Brown*

As we learn about the importance of authenticity, let me start this chapter with a story...

Once upon a time, I was an engineer in Seattle, getting ready to step out of my career so that I could get my master's degree and have my first child. But instead, through a twist of fate, in 2003 I found myself inventing a recycled-content countertop product called Squak Mountain Stone in my garage in a small bedroom community called Issaquah, Washington.

It came about as an economics paper I wrote while getting my master's. The topic was "import substitution" based on Michael Shuman's book *Going Local: Creating Self-Reliant Communities in a Global Age.* We students were tasked with looking at our own communities to find something we currently buy that was made outside of our community and to come up with an alternative. The intent was to do an exercise in understanding how keeping dollars recirculating in our neighborhoods or hometowns is better for the long-term viability of that society than it is to line the pockets of businesses based elsewhere.

Being the stunningly ambitious and painfully annoying overachiever that I am, I decided that instead of just a business paper, I would submit a business *plan*, outlining not only the product I intended to substitute, but also what kind of company would need to be created to make such a product. Now, I also decided to kick this plan up one more notch and really make it juicy. In retrospect, I have no idea why—it was grad school—it's not like I was actually getting a grade for it or an award for exceeding the parameters of the assignment. But, in any case, what I wanted was not just an economically viable substitution but one that was also a great environmental choice. And then I shot for the moon and decided I wanted it to also be socially responsible—the trifecta of true sustainability.

So, coming from the construction industry at that time, I looked at a variety of materials we used in the building of homes and businesses and decided that making a commercially viable form of an alternative recycled material known as "papercrete" was just the ticket. Being a simple mish-mash of cement, sand, and shredded newspapers, I liked papercrete for the fact that the raw ingredients are available in every community because having lived in both a big city and small town, there's one thing I know they both have in common: garbage.

Also, in my community at the time, a non-profit recycling center employed people with disabilities, and so my thought was that purchasing the shredded paper directly from them would not only keep the money in the community, but as the business grew in success, so would the benefits to this organization. I broke out the costs to make the material. I made some loose proposals about how it could be used, and then I turned my economics paper into my instructor. And for my work, I earned my pat on the back and sneers from my classmates for blowing the non-existent curve. Again.

But a funny thing happened. I couldn't stop thinking about the idea. Long after we'd moved on to a new topic, I still wondered repeatedly, "If this is such a great idea, why hasn't anyone done it yet?"

So, it started innocently, as any addiction does. First, I bought a bag of cement from the hardware store. And then I crafted a mixer from a hand-held drill and buckets after my prior attempt at converting an electric lawnmower didn't work. Then for molds, I bought a bunch of springform baking pans from the local thrift store. And since I was a stay-at-home mom, working occasionally as a green building consultant,

I would sneak out to shed in our backyard during my son's naps and begin experimenting.

I changed all kinds of variables and documented all of my tests. When my husband came home at the end of the day, I would excitedly report to him the results, and he humored me. He would be the first to admit that he did not understand my enthusiasm for what I was doing, especially since my samples looked like dusty, gray sponges. But the days and the experiments continued on and on until one day, instead of a soft spongey sample, I had something harder, almost stone-like. Curious, I grabbed a hand-sander from the toolbox and high-grit sandpaper, and I was able to polish it and make it shine. It was my eureka moment!

I started to add color and found some granite dust recycled from the blasting hopper of a local monument manufacturing company, and now samples began to look like polished limestone and slate. The shredded paper mimicked the veining you see in natural stones and after thinking about the potential uses for stone in construction, all information pointed to countertops. Then, after trying to produce full sized mock-ups in the backyard under a tent made from sheets of plastic and PVC poles, it was decided I needed a bigger garage. So, we moved. Yes, we moved because of a hunch and belief that I was finally on to something.

We didn't have to go far—just a few miles into our town of Issaquah and up into a nice neighborhood on Squak Mountain. And there, my company was born. I would spend just short of a year in the garage before moving to a real facility a few towns over and would also become pregnant during all this with my daughter. Getting help from my old childhood friend, her husband, and my husband on weekends, we started casting slabs of "Squak" for a local green building materials showroom to stock and sell. After a couple of months of beta testing with customers around the Puget Sound, some refinements to the formulation and processes, I had my first ever order ready to deliver on February 22, 2005.

Nine months pregnant and unable to fit into my forklift anymore, my husband came over during his lunch break from work to help load up the delivery truck sent by the Environmental Home Center. I had felt for weeks that I was racing against the clock of my daughter's impending birth by making sure this order and delivery was completed before then. Once the truck was loaded and on its way, I turned to my husband, rubbed my stomach, and said, "Now I can go into labor." And at midnight that night, I did.

But that was only the beginning. Learning the next steps of taking a business from invention to production forced me to teach myself everything I needed to know about business. I signed up for the Harvard Business Review email newsletter and bought just about every book they recommended related to my field. I was a quick study, an eager student, and had a hurricane-like intensity and commitment to my vision. Eighteen years ago, I was a woman who wanted to change the world just like today, only I thought it would be through the sustainable building field.

I not only learned the ins and outs of developing a manufacturing company with nationwide distribution and upwards of twenty employees, I also crafted a unique selling strategy and brand for a product that should have never existed.

But it did. And thanks to the story behind the product, I won awards, appeared on home improvement shows on HGTV and the DIY Network, and I was featured in the *Popular Mechanics* magazine.

The product and brand were both so unique that it even caught the eyes of some celebrities who were committed to supporting the cause that my company represented. In fact, supermodels to TV hosts to grunge rockers count among the customers who have Squak Mountain Stone in their homes and are members of the Squak Fan Club.

It was kind of hard not to feel like I was riding high, right up until the fall of 2009 when everything changed. No husband. No business. More about that later. I promise.

But for now, let's fast-forward a couple of years to the summer of 2011 and to a chapter in this story I've hinted around a few times in this book. In this scene, we will find me sitting on the deck of my then-boyfriend's rural home outside the Seattle area, watching a wedding play out in front of me. See, he had partnered with a local florist to host weddings on his property, and it wasn't going well—each event was losing money. They had just a few bookings and the online presence was limited. But it wasn't terrible—I could see some potential and thought it would be a completely different career for me from the heartache I had over the end of Squak Mountain Stone. And so, I thought to myself "Why not?"

I also wondered, "Can I really make lightning strike twice, but with weddings instead of countertops?"

And the answer was, "Yes."

By taking the approach I did with before and applying them to the wedding venue business, I was able to take an unknown backyard business and grow it into an award-winning six-figure company in two years. Spurred by the growth, my ex and I were able to then buy a second farm down the road. Within one year, that location would also be recognized as one of the top locations in the area.

In fact, in March of 2014, right after winning the Best of Western Washington, we had a party to celebrate. Hundreds of people showed up to the venue that hadn't even hosted a wedding yet. And then, just a couple years after that, that same venue would host a wedding with Bill Gates and his family as guests, security detail and all. I can't even begin to tell you how proud I am of that.

But by that time, I had already learned that branding and business development was one of my superpowers.

Now, I wasn't good at branding because I was an expert on the latest social media algorithms or managing robust email campaigns. In fact, when I started as an entrepreneur twenty years ago, these tools didn't even exist. It also wasn't because I was a great graphic designer and could design neat logos. No, my unique success was because I had learned how our *feelings* drive our desires to do business with some people and not others, and how important being authentic was to create those feelings.

I didn't learn this all by accident, however. My education in how emotions connect to business first started in 2006 with author Patrick Hanlon and his book *Primal Branding*. When Hanlon looked at businesses and their brands, he noticed that some companies had an almost cult-like following with customers who simply could not be persuaded to abandon the brand. And when Hanlon examined these companies, they had several things in common. One was that their brand's main features looked like the elements of religions. Further, as we all know, religions are the most powerful communities on the planet, enduring for thousands of years. And so, Hanlon's deduction was if you craft your business brand like you are creating a new religion, you just might make something that taps straight to the emotions of your followers, hence the term *Primal Branding*.

Now, always a geek myself for understanding human behavior, when I read this book back then, I loved it. Looking around and taking notes of what I was observing in my own experiences with businesses and brands, I could confirm it, and it made sense to me. So, immediately I jumped in with both feet and started applying it to my little recycled-content countertop company and every business thereafter.

HOW WE DECIDE

Unlike in 2006 when Hanlon published his book, today there are technologies that allows scientists and researchers to study how humans respond to advertising. These fields are called many things such as persuasion science, social psychology, or neuromarketing, but they are all based around understanding why people ultimately decide to do businesses with some companies but not others.

To help illustrate these important points, I'm going to borrow a couple of terms from the book *The Persuasion Code* by Dr. Christophe Morin and Patrick Renvoise. If we go back to the chapter about neuroscience, you will recall that our brain is divided to handle many functions. First, we have a portion of the brain that performs our executive functions and decision-making. That is, it takes in information and we make decisions consciously. From this point forward in the book, I want to use *The Persuasion Code* label, the **rational brain**, when talking about these functions.

Also, remember we are wired to survive and thrive. There is always an operating system in the background scanning for danger at all times, way down deep at the subconscious level—meaning we don't have to think about it because it's one of our autopilot functions. It's the part of the brain that stores important memories and triggers our emotions to help us interpret our current situations. And sometimes, depending upon our personal histories, it either assists or interferes with our rational brain when it comes to judgment and decisions. From now on, because it's the oldest part of the human brain, we'll call it the **primal brain.**

Now what researchers in the fields of advertising and marketing want to know is how do people decide when it comes to choosing Product A over Product B. And why do some people become loyal to a brand and refuse to change, even if the value proposition or features of another company are better?

To uncover this, researchers began employing cool scanning technology and software that would investigate the brains of people to see what was happening at the neurobiology level. By feeding the participants different types of advertising, they could measure what parts of the brain were lighting up and being stimulated. And they discovered time and time again, despite us all believing that we are making a rational decision about what to choose by applying logic and facts, the reality is that this isn't true. By looking at the actual parts of the brain that are stimulated, it has been shown through a variety of research studies that our primal brain is mostly in charge of decisions. That is, we decide almost instantly and below our level of consciousness whether we like something or not.

This then tells us that our marketing and branding has to connect with our customer's primal brain down deep, not the rational brain up front. And this is where authenticity comes into the picture.

A couple of years before *Primal Branding* was published, Bill George, a Harvard Business School professor and former CEO, started talking about a new form of leading in his book *Authentic Leadership: Rediscovering the Secrets to Creating Last Value*. And in this book, he described a person who was practicing authenticity as doing the five following things:

1. They are pursuing their purpose and vision with passion.
2. They are living and practicing unwavering values.

3. They are leading with their hearts and their heads.
4. They are focused on establishing positive, genuine, and connected relationships.
5. They practice and model self-discipline.

So, then what this boils down to is that once you have an understanding of who you are, what you are doing, and why it matters, you have the secret ingredients for making genuine and powerful connections with your customers. Looking at the current research and even what Hanlon wrote about years ago, if businesses and their leaders can connect with a customer's primal brain by soothing fears, inspiring trust, and creating a sense of belonging and inclusion with their customers or employees, they will have fans for life.

That's right. That's it. If you are able to generate those three feelings, you are able to persuade or influence anyone to do business with you. Sure, you can worry and fret about what to post on Facebook all day, and the latest algorithms, and if you should use a scheduling program or not, or if you should join TikTok or whatever. But none of that is as important as whether you have made a basic, human connection in some way with your potential customers. And you can't make that real connection with them unless you are real with yourself.

BECOMING AUTHENTIC

Since authenticity and authentic leadership is founded on our personal histories and understanding how our life informs our identity and our moral compass, we have to keep learning how to tease that out of ourselves in a meaningful way.

Now, your authenticity is not business specific. Meaning, once you sit down and sort out your values and your passions, which you've started to do already in this book, what you have left is applicable to any business you start or project you pursue. The difference with authentic entrepreneurship is integrating your values **into** your business and using your business as a tool to express them, not using your business as a curtain to hide behind or to pretend to be something or someone you're not.

So, to merge your authenticity with your business, I have found that it all starts with the following three steps:

1. Defining who you are and what you stand for
2. Knowing who your Haters are
3. Creating your personal narrative

DEFINING WHAT YOU STAND FOR

We're going to start with nailing down your values and your personal beliefs. They could be about life, but they should be about your reasons "why" you decided you needed to start your own company. Why do you think your product deserves to exist in the world and be available to people?

If the values your brand represents are not aligned to the values of your target customer, no amount of marketing will move them to your brand. In other words, you won't be able to hit that feeling of belonging someone will need in order to choose you. That's because, again, evidence shows that customers build an emotional connection with brands whose values align with their own, which also triggers the other primal brain feeling of trust.

This is where authenticity really matters: if the values of your brand are not aligned with you personally, you will burn out and have no reason to feel inspired to want to do the work anymore.

In fact, your primal brand can become your own rallying cry. Believing in who you are and what you stand for will sometimes be the only thing that keeps you going on bad days or when you have a bad experience. And on good days, if what you do, why you do it, and what you stand for truly gets you excited, it will show through every part of your business or job. But on the other hand, if you don't give a shit, why should anyone else?

And so, this brings us to another word you'll see in this chapter a lot: **integrity**. When you hear or see the word, most people think of its definition in terms of honesty and virtue as it applies to others. But the other meaning it has is *wholeness*, which applies to each of us.

That is, to be inspired in work and in your business, and imbue it with passion and energy, you have to understand how to live in cohesion with yourself. And where this discontinuity can happen is when you work for a business or organization that does not share your core values. When you sense and feel the misalignment, it manifests in poor work quality, a lack of motivation, and your overall demeanor. You are drained and sapped.

On the other hand, when you share values and a mutual sense of purpose to uphold those values, whether you are an employee or even a customer, your levels of inspiration and loyalty to the cause are off the charts.

EXERCISE

In this exercise, I want you to revisit some of your answers from Chapter One as well as reflect and answer these questions below:

1. What do I stand for, personally and in business? Value, affordability? Quality and workmanship? Making sure low-income people have access to what I make? Sustainable material choices?

2. What are the aspects of my life I am committed to? Family? Travel? Continuous learning?

3. What are the values, dreams, gifts, and passions I am committed to fulfilling in my life?

4. What would it take for me to live with integrity (in alignment with my true self)?

5. What kinds of people do I feel invigorated by and why?

6. What inspires me personally and professionally?

KNOWING YOUR HATERS

After sorting out your values and defining who you are and what you stand for, we're going to have some fun. See, first, we don't always feel a sense of belonging with people who all like or believe in the same things as us. Sometimes we are drawn toward others because it's what we won't stand for that is unifying. So, in further defining what makes you authentic, we're going to figure out who the **Haters** are, whether they are people who won't like what you make or do or people who don't align with your values.

Now, what I also love about figuring out who isn't going to like you is that it sets you up nicely for rejection. Weird thing to say, I know, but hear me out. You are not going to be the right fit for every customer. It's no different from when we find ourselves not wanting to be friends with everyone we meet. We have common interests and values with certain people, so it's okay that other people won't like us, right? On the other hand, too many business owners think they have to be perfect for everyone, but we all know how exhausting that really is because we can't make everyone happy.

So, when you figure out ahead of time who is definitely *not* going to like what you are doing, you get to reframe any rejections from a "they don't like me" position to an empowering "I don't like them," which tempers the burns from a cold shoulder or criticisms you will hear from people. And remember, Sisters, we are groomed to be liked and be nice to everyone, so rejection hurts. I understand. That is why this little step can be so compelling in shifting your mindset and enabling you to become comfortable setting and holding a boundary, especially around your pricing and financial worth.

Okay, now here's my secret for the best way to use this information that, yes, might feel a little like a play from the *Mad Men* playbook.

If you have been able to draw curious people in toward your business and products, and they begin to spit out some of the objections you already expected to hear, you can simply say to them, "Listen, I get it. We're not for everyone. It's okay you don't agree. I wish you luck in finding a better fit for you."

Bam! With that sentence, you just shot a cannonball into their primal brain as you've started to close the door to the clubhouse. Now in my experience, two things *always* happen at this point when someone sees you not budging. One, they agree with you and walk away which is good for you because you already know that you'll likely have problems with them. Or two, they stick their foot in the door and beg you to not shut it on them because people, by nature, don't like to be excluded or cast out.

But now, when your customer is standing at the doorway asking you if they can still join the club, you can stand there like a bouncer and tell them what the cost of admission is. Because if someone wants to join, they have to pay the cover, abide by the dress code, and behave themselves. If not, they leave, and you get to keep your business operating the way you want it with people who value and respect the same things as you.

EXERCISE

To help you understand more about what you stand for, we are going to figure out who you stand *against.* To do this, you're going to answer the following questions:

1. What kinds of people will not like my product or service? What kinds of products or services would they prefer instead?
2. What kinds of people will not understand or actually hate my values or beliefs? What do they stand for instead? Does that matter to me and why?
3. Who is going to object or complain about my pricing and why? What am I going to say to them?

CREATING YOUR NARRATIVE

The final key to unlocking your authenticity is not just acknowledging your past experiences and how they have shaped you and given you your beliefs today, but it is to also realize that your story is **evolving**. And to see life as a constantly changing journey allows us to remove the risk of being stuck in a story or role again that no longer fits us. That's why all the way back in Chapter One, I asked you start to decipher what that script might be because I know that you can't move forward if you don't let yourself outgrow your past.

Authenticity also means bringing that story out and sharing it with everyone, so that they can see you, understand you, and decide if what you are doing matters to them. And if so, they will get onboard and travel with you on your epic journey.

Now, all good stories as well as businesses that bond with their customers have a central figure—a hero. This hero is the person who has overcome extraordinary odds to bring their great idea to the world through a mythic journey. Now, not all heroes are warriors, fighting against someone or something. Sometimes, the hero in mythology is a lover or a saint, who represents beautiful ideals in the face of uncertainty or opposition and never gives up on the hope that those ideals will become more commonplace. Or maybe they just refuse to give up on themselves and their dreams.

Who cares that maybe you haven't slain any dragons or had to grow up with the odds stacked heavily against you? Maybe instead, you have this overwhelming urge to release your inner artist against the will of a society that says you "should" do something else. Perhaps you are finding the courage to break free from a career or occupation that has left you financially and maybe even emotionally bankrupt. Or maybe you are starting over in life after devastation and heartache, like a divorce or the economic collapse that resulted after the COVID-19 pandemic, and you were hellbent on finding a way to rebuild.

And so, let's go back to Chapter One and remember when you wanted to become something else when you were growing up, but you didn't. Now, let's fast-forward to right here and now and to this beautiful version of you today who's finally doing something about that. Don't sell yourself short because if you ask me, if you were willing to pick up a book that promised to make you courageous and unstoppable, then you are clearly looking to be a part of something epic!

If you recall from the start of this chapter, I told you a story about how I started my recycled-content countertop company. The whole idea for my business started about as un-heroic as it gets: it began with an economics paper and a burning question I couldn't shake. The journey and hardships were about trial and error with designs and mixes until I ended up with a piece of stone that I could polish and make beautiful. Then I knew I'd discovered a new way to make a recycled-content countertop. The end.

The challenges in my story weren't all about true villains. There were about solving problems and hopefully finding a solution to those problems. In the end, once I overcame the challenges, my return home was sharing the results with the world through my product, Squak Mountain Stone, as well as a template for starting similar types of businesses.

Now, written out, it may not sound all that epic, but to be honest, I'm pretty proud of that achievement. Not only did I invent something that didn't exist before, but I proved that triple-bottom-line businesses could really work. I became a teacher to others in the recycling world who wanted to know how to create their own companies and brands. And as a result, I ended up telling that story over and over and over again for years. It was reprinted in magazines and blog articles. I told the story at conferences, in MBA classrooms, and interviews until I was hoarse. People loved to hear it. And when I showed up sometimes to events, people loved to also tell it back to me—"You're the woman who invented this in her garage! And it was based on your economics paper, right?"

I would bet not many people have told you to sit down and write the story about your business journey, but I'm telling you it must be done. It helps reframe your history from maybe a horror story into an epic myth in which **you are the hero who saves the day**. Seeing in words how much you've been through and how far you've come helps reset the control panel in your own head, one small step at a time. Because when you write out your journey, you will realize how amazing you are and why it's so worth it for you to keep going and make your dreams come true. I also want you to learn to get into the habit of measuring yourself not by what you haven't accomplished or achieved yet, but by how far you've made it so far.

In fact, Bill George even said, "To be effective leaders of people, authentic leaders must first discover the purpose of their leadership... To discover their purpose, authentic leaders have to understand themselves and the passions that animate their life stories."

So, let's write your new narrative.

EXERCISE

Using the framework of classical myths, as notably identified by writer Joseph Campbell in his 1949 book *The Hero with a Thousand Faces*, I want you to think about each statement below and then fill in your own information. This doesn't have to be your entire life story, so if it helps, think of either a recent period or series of events that lead you to decide to start your business.

Our Hero receives a call to adventure and embarks on the Journey. When and where does your story begin? Was it when you left home to go to college? Or did your call to adventure happen a little closer to home in the form of inspiration in a class or from meeting a certain person and having a life-changing conversation? Did your journey begin during the pandemic or during another terrible loss, like a death or divorce?

Our Hero faces many challenges and has to fight a few battles, not all successful, but finally, victory is won. What are some of the struggles you encountered on your personal journey? Were you trying to find a solution to a problem? Did you have to experiment and fail a few times? Did you actually end up doing something you didn't love for a while until you had an eye-opening moment or event? Did you have people discount you and tell you it couldn't be done? How did you finally win your victory?

Returning home with new powers and sharing them with others. This where you are now, likely: starting your business so that you can share your life lessons with others. Or perhaps you are still in the "challenges" stage of your mythic adventure. That's okay too! If that's the case, say so and tell everyone you're as excited about the ending as they are!

This might seem like a short exercise, but I'm here to tell you that beginning to have a narrative of your life and the moments leading up to you wanting to get into entrepreneurship is not only a key piece of the brand you'll ultimately create, but it will ground you in more ways than you realize. Again, people are more likely to achieve their goals when they know why they are doing it. And when you can also begin to see that you really are the hero in your own story who is fighting for what you believe in, you are well on your way to developing the courage you need to keep going and becoming unstoppable.

WHY BECOMING AUTHENTIC IS HARD

Now comes the hard part for most people when it comes to public displays of authenticity: being vulnerable and facing rejection of who we are. Remember that we are herd creatures, and we believe we are safest when in the company of others like us, so authenticity is scary if we think that nobody else believes in the same things. Too many women were taught that their needs didn't matter growing up. Sometimes, the consequences of trying to be our true selves were harsh, bitter, and painful. And that really sucks. For many of us, people telling us to "tone it down" or be "nice" robbed us of our courage to be authentic.

There is something else that makes it difficult for many women to imagine themselves as the hero and leader of their own stories, and that is crippling doubt. All those voices that discredited us or told us to do something different planted seeds in our heads that who we really are isn't good enough. I mentioned this earlier in the money chapter, that research has shown that women have low levels of entitlement and downplay their own accomplishments far more than men do.

Noting a pattern of behavior in people who, despite evidence to the contrary, still remained convinced they didn't deserve success, two clinical psychologists, Pauline Clance and Suzanne Imes, coined the term **imposter syndrome**.

Imposter syndrome is not actually a mental health disorder, but it is a powerful influence on the lives of many women. And I mention it here because after giving you the instructions on how to write a Hero's Journey with you in the starring role, I would bet many of you started to feel a little weird about it. You might have chalked up some of your successes to just being lucky. Or writing a heroic story made you feel like you are a fraud, and then you didn't want to share it with anyone, or risk being discovered and publicly embarrassed. I know that feeling. It's fucking scary.

In any case, if we get out of own heads for a minute, we can usually see that the evidence is there that our accomplishments and victories are earned and well-deserved. And we will see that these feelings are pretty normal for most people because, as I have presented several times so far, we all have a bit of a messed-up childhood sprinkled in that can cause these feelings of doubts to seem like facts.

So, to fight against imposter syndrome, you can start by rereading your personal myth and remind yourself of all you have achieved. And you can look through this book for the evidence that the voices inside of us are not telling us the truth, they are there to scare us out of changing.

We are going to keep working on this as we move into the next chapter because being authentic is scary and building our courage is vital.

WHY INTEGRITY MATTERS

I am going to end the chapter with the sad tale of how the awesome little manufacturing business I started in my garage almost twenty years ago died.

As I wrote this section, it brought back a surprising amount of grief all these years later. And it is not lost on me that many of you reading this book may have lost a company already due to the COVID-19 pandemic in a similar way.

First, a brand that is truly authentic is deeply connected to a business and person and it is a living and breathing thing, like a human. As you and your business grow, it's like being a teenager struggling to individuate and discover who you are. You may start out with a lot of ideas of what you want and how you should be, but you will find along the way that through a very organic process, what feels right will naturally come out.

Companies also become families in the sense that the interplay of our nervous systems all become a factor as well.

So, it goes without saying that as you hire people and bring them into your company, your culture will evolve as well. When I started my recycled-content countertop company, I worked many days alone in my backyard shed. And then when I took it another step and needed help, my friend, her husband, and my husband joined me on the weekends. This mini-version of my company had a culture of sorts, but it was a couple of years later, as I brought on full-time employees— mostly young men who reminded me of my troubled younger brothers, that the true personality of the company emerged and central to this culture were my strong values regarding second chances.

For one, I didn't believe it was fair to be passionately committed to upcycling a piece of garbage if we weren't willing to do the same for people. So, most of my employees had some problems or concerns that made them difficult to employ with other companies. I had standards in my business regarding performance and a requirement that these young men must be living in a way that their past was going to stay behind them. And if they complied with those two things, and if they wanted a future, it could be with me.

Some of my guys figured it out and were dedicated and loyal while others who didn't were swiftly addressed. It was tough to stay with me in my company if you didn't follow through on changing for the better, but for those who did—man, we were an awesome little family. Me and my surrogate little brothers—the brothers I *could* save.

On the outside, however, this crew of mine looked a bit rough. And some of them were! But I didn't realize how we looked to others until one day one of the guys came into the shop after his smoke break in the alley. He had been sharing his time with some of the employees at the auto body shop across the way and said that the auto body shop had nicknamed us "Convict Countertops" on account of how scary some of the employees looked with their neck tattoos and such. We loved it and I even had T-shirts made.

I then stood back and reevaluated what my company's personality had grown into, from all different aspects. We were just on the cusp of securing nationwide distribution and the time was right to really solidify the Squak Mountain Stone brand. But it was also becoming clearer who we really were and what we stood for:

- We stood for second chances—for materials and people.
- We stood for the Japanese principle of wabi-sabi—beauty in age and in imperfection.
- We were "counterculture"—we were misfits making products that were bucking the trends.
- We were the underdogs—the product and people others underestimated.
- We showed through our lives that you can't always judge a book by its cover.
- And finally, we were proof that when you do give someone or something a second chance, they can come back more beautiful than before, tattoos, rap music, shredded paper, and all.

And I ran with it. And it worked. Not only did it give a great story for our dealers and distributors to tell, but my guys felt it all and believed it because it was true and we became stronger and stronger as a team. And then my guys became the best filter for new employees I could have. When their friends begged to join the company, they knew what it took and they too didn't want to see it spoiled, so they'd say "no" before I even had to. We became powerful together, joined by what was more than just a "brand," but it was truly who we were as a team. A family. It was us against the world. And when the company crossed the five-year mark in 2008, we celebrated the fact that we beat the odds and made it longer than most businesses ever do.

So, when the Recession came upon us just a year later in the fall of 2009, it was like a cold, harsh wind that kicked up out of nowhere.

One month, I had a six-figure offer from one of my distributors to buy my company, and the very next month, that same distributor was going bankrupt. I had to weigh devasting, unfair choices, and one was to decide if I should shut my company down and let everyone go. My husband at the time would soon become my ex because he pushed to end it and I insisted on going. I could not see how breaking up my family and letting my dream die was even an option on the table. My vision for what I imagined everything could be was powerful and unfulfilled, so I was dedicated to surviving the Recession by any means necessary.

And then, by a stroke of luck or the magic of the Universe or a little bit of both, another choice came into my life just a month later. I was approached by another company who had been unable to bring their product to market but had significant financial resources to ride out the storm.

They wanted to form a partnership. Despite the wobble of uncertainty in my gut, I signed the papers and had a new business partner. I had just made sure my guys were still employed but with fear driving me, I gave up 85 percent of my interest in my company to do it.

But the sad irony was that the company I had built was dead the moment I signed the papers. The new partner had his own ideas on what our "culture" and brand needed to be. And even though the entire business was centered on my products, my employees, my customers, and my fans, and I was still the CEO, the introduction of something new caused our family dynamic to shift.

Trying to describe what it felt like, all I could think of was it was like we'd added a new stepdad who was a former Army general and he thought all the Lost Boys needed to straighten up and be more like him. But that wasn't all. My partner and I also had differences in how to treat people we worked with outside of our company, like our vendors and business customers. My partner and I did not share the same core values or moral compass. He'd gotten into recycled building materials because it was the new cool fad and he wanted to make a few bucks from it. You all, however, know I was inspired to start for an entirely different reason.

It would have been easier in the long run if I had just decided to close it all down in 2009. I would have grieved and then moved on. But instead, I had to endure the torture of watching everything I'd built go through a slow, painful death. It changed me. I felt the strain of living inauthentically and out of integrity with myself. My guys grew unhappy because their "big sister" was unhappy. And then, in less than two years, we had all scattered to the wind like dandelions, and two years after that, the badass little company I started in my garage almost ten years earlier was gone and so was my marriage.

Living outside of integrity was a dark toxin that poisoned me. As I fought against the changes with my partner, it made the situation worse between us. Maybe, in hindsight, something else could have been done, but I was operating with the levels of awareness I had then. And looking back to that time, it was definitely the beginning of a long, hard journey of growth for me that I'd have to endure for another seven years.

This is how powerful this is, this concept of knowing who you are and what you stand for and shaping the heart of your business around it. I say this many times when speaking or coaching or just shooting the shit with people while having a beer: being an entrepreneur means you are **consumed** by your idea and your reason "why." You are about to will into existence something that never lived before on this planet. It is very much like giving birth. And just like there are other humans on this earth, there may be other businesses like yours, but they are not yours. Yours will be and should be unique. And it should be something you are proud of and dedicated to, like any mother with her child.

I swore after that experience to do many things differently. One was to never put myself into a situation where I am asked to change who I fundamentally am and what I truly value. And so, one of my core values today is that regardless of the personal or professional relationship, I must have a shared connection with the people and the organization. It's too costly if I or anyone else allows anything less.

Chapter Six

BECOMING COURAGEOUS: COMMUNICATE WITH CONFIDENCE

"A woman with a voice is by definition a strong woman. But the search to find that voice can be remarkably difficult."

–Melinda Gates

So, let's start this chapter with this question: why does it seem that men don't have the same issue of speaking up and getting what they want? Is it because we really are biologically different?

The biological or evolutionary theories about why women may be more nurturing, emotionally involved, and agreeable are centered around reproduction and having a parental investment in raising children. While in this realm, because men have an ability to procreate more often, they are then biologically driven to obtain as many mating opportunities as possible, so they will be more assertive, risk-taking, and even aggressive.

I can buy that. I mean, while there is a lot about neuroscience that we now know, I am smart enough to also realize that there is still a lot we don't know. So, I'm going to keep an open mind.

But there is the indisputable research that shows that communication is also shaped by parenting and culture, and people are socialized to behave certain ways as well. How do we know this? Well, if it was purely biological, then we'd have no control over how we communicate, and yet, there are **cultural differences** worldwide between how men and women communicate.

However, there is also another universal theme that is too hard to ignore which I brought up the chapter about money disorders: women do not believe they are good enough when, in fact, they are. And men, on the other hand, think they are better than they are. And the delta between those two sentiments is what we see in salary gaps, promotions, power, and an overall lack of parity between genders. But why is that?

In an internet study of one million people in forty-eight countries, researchers looked at gender differences in self-esteem, a marker for how assertive a person may be, and found steadily **in each culture, without exception,** women consistently and significantly rated themselves lower than men when asked their degree of agreement with this

216

statement, "I see myself as someone who has high self-esteem."

Now, this is a chapter where I am going to fight my urge to over-explain the reasons our abilities to stand up for ourselves feel so hard and focus a great deal instead on overcoming those fearful feelings and building courage. And again, because confidence is going to be such a big part of becoming courageous, we must learn to trust ourselves more. That means, in turn, learning how to shut off the false voices in our heads that constantly raise doubts about our worth, value, or our abilities.

So, I want to talk about why your courage was stolen and how we are born to push and explore our world so that we can learn. We were born to ask questions and become independent, but somewhere along the way for many, many women, we were taught something different. We were told our questions were silly. That our needs made us selfish. That our voices were too loud and that if we kept talking like that, no one would like us. And unfortunately, we believed them.

WHO TAUGHT US HOW TO TALK

Let us start back at the beginning of this book and the conversation about brain building and how the architecture of our minds is formed. If you remember, I presented the concept of serve and return and how that is the primary way a child's brain—our brains—learns about their world and develops interpersonal skills.

When researchers began to turn their attentions toward children and human behavior in the early parts of the twentieth century, some began to see patterns emerging. One was a British psychoanalyst John Bowlby who noted the patterns of interfamily relationships that were involved in healthy and unhealthy emotional development in the children he took care of as a physician. But it would be his student, Mary Ainsworth, who would run her own research projects based on Bowlby's theory that would cement the entire theory of **attachment** and attachment styles.

According to attachment theory, attachment is the process where infants seek out a responsive, secure attachment figure for safety and support when they are in distress. This attachment period appears to happen very early in the infant's life between six months to two years of age. If, during the brain-building actions of serve and return, a child has a sensitive and responsive adult who is consistent, then that child will form a healthy, **secure** attachment with their caregiver. If a child, on the other hand, has an unresponsive adult or one who is inconsistent, the child forms insecure attachments.

What the research has shown over the past five decades is that these parental responses lead to the internal scripts that will then guide a person's emotional growth as well as their feelings, thoughts, and expectations in all of their later relationships, from romantic to friendships to business. Also, by studying adults, researchers have seen that the type of attachments we develop remains stable over our lifetime. In fact, our attachment style informs those personality traits we develop that I told you about a few chapters back.

Today, based on the original and subsequent theories, the four basic styles of attachment observed in children and adults are *secure, anxious-ambivalent, fearful-avoidant, and dismissive-avoidant.*

A person who formed a **secure** attachment style with their caregiver is comfortable with establishing close emotional bonds. They also exhibit a healthy balance of relying on other people while being independent. It is knowing that people can be a safe anchor that allows secure people to develop healthy confidence, self-esteem, and an ability to bounce back. In the end, they don't carry a deep-seated fear of being rejected or abandoned by people.

People who have an **anxious-ambivalent** style, on the other hand, worry constantly about being rejected or abandoned and respond by becoming clingy. In extreme cases, this can lead to controlling behaviors and possessiveness. An anxious person tends to carry a poor self-image and low self-confidence and assumes that everyone will leave or reject them, even when things are going fine. This style can happen when a parent was inconsistent and unreliable, leaving a child to question constantly whether their parent would show up or not and feeling unloved when they didn't.

Now, people with a **fearful-avoidant** attachment style also fear being abandoned or rejected, but instead of clinging on, they run away or distance themselves. Sadly, they have learned that people can't be trusted and that it's safer to scan for danger and steer clear. While they may appear to be uncaring, the reality is that they have a fear of not being loved if they try to form an emotional connection. So, then sometimes a fearful person will become a self-saboteur in relationships by creating hurdles to closeness so that the rejection becomes a self-fulfilling prophecy. This style can happen from unresponsive parenting, which leaves a child feeling unworthy.

The final attachment style, the **dismissive-avoidant**, is the one most commonly maligned in pop psychology relationship articles because these people do not live in fear of being abandoned or rejected and generally have no desire to develop close relationships to others. What they do fear, however, is being overwhelmed by someone's emotional needs and will actively avoid people who appear to be too needy. Unlike the fearful-avoidant, people with this style tend to have higher levels of self-esteem and a strong belief in their own abilities because they had to learn to be self-reliant and built up confidence in themselves. And while they may want to have a loving relationship with another person, they are extremely picky because they need to have their own space. This attachment style happens when a child regularly doesn't feel safe, seen, or soothed by their parent. Therefore, they become independent because they've learned that they can't depend on people who consistently failed them. And to avoid the shame that they weren't good enough to be cared for by their parents, a self-protective disdain for emotional closeness develops instead.

This last style is the bucket I landed in, by the way. And it's expressed in my life by the fact I have a very small circle of people I am close to. I am aware that I tend to be attracted to people who will not overwhelm me with their emotional needs, not just romantically, but also in friendships. It is also probably why in my professional career, I have been more comfortable in male-dominated fields because, sadly, men have been groomed to be more independent.

However—and this is the part that always blows my mind—I was trapped in an emotionally abusive relationship for many years. That is because a partner who happens to have dark traits like psychopathy, extreme jealousy, or narcissism can push the buttons in an emotional control panel that triggers a person's deepest fears—abandonment. And while the needle on my attachment style remained avoidant, there was this toxic shroud that began to envelope me called **codependency.**

Unlike the attachment styles we just covered, codependency is an added flavor of interpersonal behavior where people are attracted to others who need "saving." They rely heavily on the approval of others to confirm their personal identity, always at their own well-being and expense. And as my case demonstrates, while it appears to be the behavior one would see in a people-pleasing anxious person, in fact, it can happen to anyone. That is because this behavior goes back to understanding our family roles. This is about having played the role of hero in our families.

What does codependency have to do with communication styles and business? Well, codependency is about putting your own needs on the back burner because your job is to take care of someone else. And it also means that you are overlooking this other person's troubles or even making excuses for them while they continue to use you. And the kicker is, as a codependent, you know you shouldn't do any of those things, but you can't seem to stop.

In business, it means you're the person who thinks if you keep working harder, you can overcome your coworker's slack performance and your boss will notice, not realizing your teammates are taking advantage of you. Or if you have a partner who is misbehaving with the company's money, you figure you can make up for it by doing your job better or being a good example for them, instead of just cutting them out or walking away.

So, now I also want to circle back to discussion we had earlier about **differentiation.** Remember that through our experiences with our family and the interconnected, dynamic system we lived in, we learned something about how our emotions interplayed with others and what was allowed or not allowed in terms of expressing them. We also learned that families with disfunction in communication developed roles for everyone to play. Therefore, ultimately how we learned the rules of communication and expressing our needs is, in part, based on the attachment relationship we had with caregivers and the role we were assigned in the family drama. And remember, the more often we repeat a behavior or see it modeled for us, the stronger the connection becomes in our brain.

"BOSSY" WOMEN V. THE WORLD

Now for some more bad news. Understanding our communication styles and how they evolved from what we learned in our families might not still be enough to inspire courage in ourselves. And that is because despite the evidence that not speaking up hurts us emotionally and financially, we are punished for trying to change that through microaggressions, which I mentioned in the money chapter.

First, I find it hypocritical that we idealize women as being more in touch with the emotional aspects of life and having a greater sense of empathy than men, but when women want to express all of these emotions or do anything other than coddle another person, they are put down or penalized for it. This, in turn, has lowered our self-esteem or made us believe our needs don't matter.

I mean, when have you ever been congratulated or thanked for letting someone know how angry you were so that they could help you through it? Or when did someone pat you on the back because you came to them for help, not the other way around?

No, we have been heralded for being the carriers and defenders of everyone else's needs and feelings by making sure we never communicated our own. That is the true, extremely one-sided "feminine ideal"—it is always about them. It is never about us.

It is no wonder, sadly, why women have turned into empathy Jedis, then. We have had little choice. Back in the earlier chapters, I gave you the statistics that women suffer more adversities in childhood than men. That means we have grown up with more dysfunction and therefore have a highly tuned radar for the emotions of the people around us, due to our survival needs.

And if we did not acknowledge and respect the emotions of those around us, we were punished for it. If we did not learn how to keep ours in check, we were punished for it. We are exactly as you would expect us to be given the circumstances—warm, compassionate, empathetic, and selfless—to the detriment of ourselves.

While it's easy to think this is about men versus women here, think again. We **all** perpetuate these stereotypes about how a woman should behave. Yes, women punish other women who try to break free from the "herd" as well. I know you've seen it happen.

Am I making this up? Is this all really that bad you ask?

Yes, it really is. Research after research, study after study, all confirm that **worldwide** women have lower levels of confidence, self-worth, and no desire to rock the boat. I mentioned that before and I'm going to mention it again because it's that important.

In fact, in one report I read from the University of Houston, the researchers wanted to understand how to bridge the gap between men and women's confidence levels and found that women seemed to perceive the backlash from standing up for one's needs or speaking confidently as **worse** than any benefit they received for being assertive. So, they keep their mouths shut because they thought it was better than to suffer the consequences. And sometimes that is the motherfucking truth. It is better to stay quiet.

So, you learned in one chapter about self-destructive money behaviors we may have that keep us as underearners, but now do you want to learn another fucked up fact about women, business, and money?

Research has proven that for women in the working world, even entrepreneurs, there is a real penalty to raising your hand and saying something. In fact, in a 2015 research study by VitalSmarts, they confirmed what other studies have shown which is that gender bias is a real thing in the workplace. Their research found that if a woman asserted herself, she was called "aggressive," her perceived competency dropped by 35 percent, and her perceived deserved annual compensation dropped by over $15,000 per year!

The reasons behind this might come from the results of another study by Victoria Brescoll and Eric Uhlmann, "Can an Angry Woman Get Ahead?" published in 2008 where they found that when a woman expresses a negative emotion like anger—whether they are a CEO or entry-level trainer—they were looked down upon by men and women alike.

The researchers found a woman's expression of anger was attributed to their internal character or a personality "flaw" with terms like "she is an angry person" or "she's out of control." But on the other hand, the study showed that when men expressed anger, the study participants provided external reasons for the man's emotional state, excusing it and letting it go without damage to his status or reputation.

Here's the thing: men and woman all feel the same things and, as research also shows, there really isn't that big of a difference between the personalities of men and women. That means that there are just as many warm, empathetic, and people-pleasing men as there are driven, confident, and outspoken women—and everyone in between. The only difference is we have gender personality stereotypes of how "real men" and "real women" should behave based largely on how we were raised. So, you can see that if we don't change our parenting culture, these stereotypes will continue.

But the world is changing, right? I mean there seem to be examples of strong, assertive women in positions of power. And what about all these corporate brands pushing female empowerment now? Yeah, about that.

In a research study published in 2017 from the Geena Davis Institute on Gender in Media at Mount Saint Mary's University and J. Walter Thompson New York found that while some advertisers love to create marquee campaigns targeting female empowerment, nothing has changed in ten years.

The reality is, even as we become more "aware" and empowered, the study showed that men still get about four times as much screen time as women and speak about seven times more than women. Furthermore, there are usually twice as many male characters as female ones. And only 5 percent of ads feature women, including women of color, only with less than 3 percent featuring female voices only.

"What this research shows is that our industry has 'tent-pole moments'—amazing actions or campaigns when we all rally around women," says Brent Choi, chief creative officer of J. Walter Thompson New York, "but when it comes to creating our 'regular' ads for our 'regular' clients, we forget about them."

This means we are still given ongoing, subtle messages that reinforce the idea that men speak and women listen. The study also revealed that men are shown in the media significantly more as leaders while women, on the other hand, are shown at home.

Remember, while what we see (or don't see) today is important for shifting mindsets and attitudes, what is really most important is what we've *already learned* because that is everything our current primal brain operating systems are based on. Like everything else I've been telling you in this book, fighting against the systemic and historic hurdles that make women disadvantaged in business does not start in the outside world, it starts in our inner worlds. That is the only thing we have complete control over changing.

OUR COMMUNICATION STYLES

So, when we add up the information about what our personal attachment style is and how much our families modeling impacted us and how society treats us, where do we end up? Well, since the brain loves to keep things simple and to automate, when we have a default pattern of interacting with people, we end up with a default pattern of communication.

How do we uncover this pattern? Well, the first place to look for cues to what these are will be in the personality tests I recommended you take. Today's tests actually integrate into them the principles of attachment theory and can predict very well what your communication patterns are without telling you straight up what your relationship with your parent was like. Because who wants to have *that* awkward conversation with HR?

But when you take the results of an attachment style test (link in the Appendix) and overlay it with your personality test, you actually begin to see the roots and sources of those strong behaviors you demonstrate in life and at work. In fact, when the personality tests are telling you what your natural communication styles are and how others likely perceive you, they are, in a sense, giving you some insights into your attachment style. And you will probably develop a bit more compassion for yourself too.

Now, when we talk about communication, I would like you to remember that it doesn't happen in a vacuum. Communication, again, is not just what you say but how you say it and how the others hear it. You have to view how and why you communicate as a part of a dynamic, living system, affected greatly by the other members of the conversation. So, let's review the most common patterns of dysfunctional communication. As you read them, think about if you ever use any of them and when.

THE SHEEP: PEOPLE-PLEASING OR PASSIVE

This is the pattern used by people who have learned to avoid expressing their opinions or standing up for their rights, needs, or wants. It the style most used by people who are anxiously attached, but that's not always the case.

This communication style is also used by women who are trying to avoid the penalties from microaggression, especially around men. Unfortunately, this style then reinforces the belief that someone who behaves this way is a "team player" everyone thinks is "nice," making it harder to stop engaging this way or risk the consequences. But some Sheep have learned that this pattern has a dark benefit: if you never speak up and express an opinion, then everyone else is to blame when something goes wrong. Or, better yet, you are not responsible for your own problems because you let others tell you what to do.

Finally, people who have developed this pattern of communication also do not speak up in situations that are hurtful or make them angry because they may have learned that it was dangerous to say anything or they just want to run away. So, instead, they let all the feelings build up inside of them until they burst. This outburst may happen during a meeting or they discharge it all afterwards. Sadly, after the outburst, they might feel guilty or ashamed of their behavior and can slip back into being a Sheep.

THE WOLF: DOMINATE OR AGGRESSIVE

Looking first at the definition of aggressive, it is very clear, linguistically speaking, that we are talking about actions or behaviors that are intended to dominate or encroach on other people's needs in a hostile or destructive way. That is why this label is so dangerous to be nonchalantly used to describe women who are not actually a Wolf but are just not acting like a Sheep.

In the truer meaning of the word, the aggressive style of communication is used by a person who expresses their needs and opinions in ways that violate the rights of others. This is done by abusive means such as blaming, interruptions, and name-calling. While studies do show a strong correlation between a hostile or dominate personality and the avoidant attachment style, the Wolf inside can also pop out of a Sheepish person after they've had it with being walked all over, as I mentioned earlier.

However, the Wolf, like the Sheep, is a communication style based on survival and protection from dysfunction. So, if the Sheep is the communication version of "flight," then the Wolf is the communication version of "fight." And so, people can also become Wolfish if they have become triggered and instead of taking a breath or a little time before reacting, they bare their teeth, and you hear an uncharacteristic growl. Unfortunately, once the Wolf appears, either in yourself or someone else, usually the whole flock's fight-or-flight system has been kicked on and the rational brain has been benched so that the primal brain can take over, which means your meeting is over.

THE BLACK SHEEP: PASSIVE-AGGRESSIVE

The Black Sheep could also be called the Wolf in Sheep's clothing because someone who is passive-aggressive appears to be quiet and compliant but really is acting out in hostile ways behind the scenes. These people are full of resentment but have developed a pattern based on the belief that they cannot deal directly with the object of their resentment, so they feel powerless and stuck.

Therefore, they rely on subterfuge and undermining others through subtle and indirect means like sarcasm, muttering, or gossip. Black Sheep might also make jokes at other people's expense in meetings and when confronted, pass them off with, "Chill. I was only kidding."

Black Sheep, unfortunately, suffer from self-sabotage because usually everyone else recognizes their behavior for what it is. And as the name implies, the Black Sheep is kept at a distance from the rest of the flock. Professionally, this means their ideas aren't taken seriously or they are excluded from decisions. They might also have poor work and personal relationships because people don't trust them or get tired of the negative comments. This in turn becomes the self-fulfilling prophecy and reinforces the Black Sheep's victim mentality.

Now, it is very likely that with different people, your communication style shifts because we discriminate how we are going to engage with people based on the power dynamic between us. Lara Currie, a corporate trainer who works with organizations in high-conflict fields, identifies these dynamics as falling into three areas: power, peer, or pupil.

What happens is that when we engage with someone, our subconscious begins to assess the situation and the person to try to figure the best and safest ways to interact. If we were raised in dysfunction and are speaking with a person that we perceive or know has **power** over us, we tend to freeze first. Then, our brain starts to decipher the posture or "danger level" of this person before we decide the safest way to respond. And depending on our fear levels, we may choose to become more Sheepish than we might otherwise be with other people.

Now, when it comes to someone who's a **peer** to us, like a coworker or our friends, we don't have problems pushing the envelope a little and testing boundaries because we are seeking equality with them. Lara describes it as a dance where you could bounce around from passive to assertive to aggressive and back again as your brain sorts out what's working and what's not. Also, it is not unusual that some people tend to be Wolfish at home around close friends and family because they feel like they have to be Sheepish at work. So, these people discharge their negative feelings to people they feel safe to do so with. I'm not saying that's healthy, but we all know it happens.

Finally, when we are around people who we perceive to have power over, or **pupils**, depending on our character and history, we might take one of two directions. First, we might feel it is our responsibility to protect them in a parent-like way and our engagement might actually look a lot like the way we had wished we were parented as a child. On the other hand, again, depending on your experiences and where you are in terms of understanding them, you might find yourselves behaving more Wolfish and looking to take on an even more powerful position and make yourself the indisputable alpha.

The goal is that, once you become aware of your communication styles, you can catch yourself when you slip into one of the unhealthy patterns and start to ask yourself, "Wait, why am I suddenly ready to give up my rights or needs? What is going on with this person that's making me feel like I have to behave this way?"

BECOMING A SHEPHERD

If most of the people we meet in life have some degree of dysfunction, and they have adapted accordingly, then most of our meetings or gatherings will have a variety of Sheep, Black Sheep, and sometimes some wolves. And if that is the case, then these flocks need Shepherds to help them feel safe and get them to where they need to go.

Now, if some of you had a decently secure childhood or some solid self-awareness skills building, then what I'm about to cover might not be that foreign to you. But even people who can comfortably express their needs and set healthy boundaries don't always get what they want. Because, again, revisiting a point I made earlier—communication is not only about what you say but about what the other person hears. So, a Shepherd knows that in the end, they can't control other people, they can only control themselves. And that when they don't get what they want, it isn't an attack against their self-esteem or self-worth.

But communicating like a Shepherd is so much more than becoming a woman who can speak up in a meeting or small talk at a networking event. We are talking about having the most fundamental skill of all that is required to be a courageous, authentic, and unstoppable entrepreneur. Because in the end, if you can't say what you mean or need, your business will not survive, let alone thrive. And so, through thousands of words on dozens of pages, I have been giving you the ultimate handbook on **social intelligence**.

First, social intelligence is the ability to know yourself and to know others. The research indicates that those who can deal with changing, complex social situations and gain power, influence, and status are the ones who exhibit high social intelligence skills. And being a businessowner is being a complex social situation, is it not?

The key, however, is that to master and grow your social intelligence, you have to have pretty high levels of self-awareness or cognition of what drives you to begin with. This is why I have continued to point out how our brains work and why we do the things we do in a variety of ways and situations.

Then after you've begun to decipher yourself, you apply that knowledge and awareness to the people around you. It's doesn't mean you start to label and diagnose your friends, coworkers, and family's mental disorders. What it does mean you pick up on the facts that they are like you, in the sense they are also driven by the same neurological functions you are.

Finally, the last part of social intelligence is taking all that awareness of yourself and others and coming up with how you will respond, not in your typical reactive way but in a thoughtful, purposeful way.

Therefore, becoming a Shepherd means you must learn and develop all the following skills, which I have been helping you do throughout this book:

1. Knowing yourself such as your fears, triggers, communication weaknesses, and strengths and be constantly applying this knowledge to your conversations or interactions with others.
2. Knowing and understanding other people and what makes them tick.
3. Being skilled in communication and saying what you need to say, verbally or in writing.

4. Reading situations and being aware of how others see you and knowing what role or script you should be following in order to successfully navigate the situation and get the outcome you want.

And so, let's review some of key social intelligence strategies Shepherds use to do this.

LISTENING IS FOR LEARNING

Shepherds know that the golden rule in communication is if you want to be heard, you have to be willing to listen.

So, being a great listener not only validates the other person and honors their rights to be heard, but Shepherds know that if they spend the time listening to another person, they can usually learn about that person's inner world. This will give insight into their pains and needs and help you understand how you or your business can take care of them.

Spending the time in listening mode isn't only about hearing what they are saying but using that time to watch for everyone's non-verbal communication such as their body language or inflections in their speech. It is important to learn the skills of figuring out when a person's threat detection system has been turned on because it can impact the overall success of a conversation or negotiation. If you have people you work with regularly, knowing each person's demeanor becomes really valuable for you as a leader or mentor because again, it will give you clues as to when you need to make a shift or adjustment.

When it comes to listening to what other people are saying, there is a practice called **active listening**. This is where you reflect or repeat back to someone what you think you heard them say. This allows you to make sure that you have, in fact, understood what was being said so that there are no misunderstandings. But it also has a secondary benefit of forming trust with the other person because you have just told them that you are genuinely listening to them and making an effort to understand them.

Another tactic that Shepherds use is to open a meeting with a question that allows for the other person or persons to express their pains and needs right away while you listen. When you have given the floor to everyone to make their own feelings and concerns heard first, then you have opened the door for you to come in with your solutions to solve their pains. It also helps you locate the landmines early in the discussion rather than to accidentally step on them later.

READ THE ROOM

Going back to the brain and our stress-response system—and thinking about every fight we've ever had with our siblings, parents, friends, boyfriends, or girlfriends and on and on—did anything ever get solved when both of you were amped up on emotions? No.

Same happens at work. So, when something happens that bothers or triggers you, Shepherds know it is a good idea to wait until your own emotions are soothed enough for you to have a calmer, wise conversation with the other person.

Not only will this help you perhaps get your meaning and concerns expressed more clearly on your part, but Shepherds realize how approaching someone while in a calm, controlled state decreases the chance of accidentally setting off everyone else's alarms.

Shepherds also know that some people have difficulties making decisions on the spot and need extra time, so it may be possible to build into a decision-making process some time for everyone to think about it and then get back together.

Additionally, Shepherds are mindful of the externalities that could be influencing the person they need to speak with and what impact that could have on them. That could be mean not forcing an agenda or timeline onto someone who could be really busy or stressed with other things. A Shepherd knows that forcing the conversation can backfire.

Now, if someone's alarm has been pulled, a Shepherd knows how to push the pause button on it in a way that doesn't drop the subject altogether but does quickly allow for the airspace someone might need. This means not ending a heated moment with "You and I are going to talk about what you did later!"—like your parents may have barked at you after you came home late. But more like, "I see that it's getting tense here and so I suggest we take a break for a moment and then come back to this, okay?"

Therefore, being observant of non-verbal cues in other people is critical. Many times, I have called a meeting off when I could see one person begin to flush and then posture themselves as if they were trying to retreat but were feeling trapped in their seat. Whatever was being discussed did not matter to them anymore because they were shutting down and it wasn't fair, in my opinion, to continue.

In the end, Shepherds feel a sense of obligation to ensuring safety, communality, and respect for everyone's rights, so that sometimes does mean showing leadership in a tough situation by pulling the plug.

DIFFUSE BOMBS BEFORE THEY GO OFF

Sometimes you have to deliver a message or tell someone something they are not going to want to hear. When you do that, you risk the arousal of the negative emotions that drive the person *away* from what you want or need from them. Shepherds know and anticipate that.

Using a theory about emotions developed by American psychologist Robert Plutchik, the persuasion scientist who wrote *The Persuasion Code* I mentioned in the last chapter, developed a process for creating the **emotional lift** you want for someone to pay attention to, so that they can jumpstart the decision-making part of their primal brain.

What they found as the most effective way of doing this is to first address an avoidance emotion such as fear, sadness, disgust, or anger, by reminding the person you're speaking to of their pain. Then, follow with an approach emotion, like joy, anticipation, or trust that lets them experience the gain of your solution or proposition.

For example, think of all the times someone asks you, "What do you want first—the good news or the bad news?" And what do people typically say? "Give me the bad news first."

So, this pre-frame lets you tackle the negative right away and gets the person's attention so that when you deliver the solution, they are more likely to accept it. Researchers found another upside for women who do this.

In the same research study by VitalSmarts I mentioned earlier this chapter, the researchers found that brief **framing statements** can go a long way toward reducing the backlash related to women speaking up assertively. In fact, their research measured the impacts as a reduction of 27 percent. They also suggested in their white paper that by leading an assertive statement with a pre-framing statement, the anticipated negative perception of the statement was significantly reduced.

This is because framing statements all provide a runway to the assertive comment that follows, taking away any surprises or hits to the fight-or-flight responses people may have that pushes the topic straight down into the primal brain. A good pre-frame is a lot like foreshadowing in horror film, giving you time to grab your blanket so that you can cover your face as fast as possible.

In my experience, pre-frames have been one of the most effective tools I have used in business communication. On one side, it allows you to be authentic, for example, "I'm feeling myself get really frustrated right now, and so it's possible that what I say might come in a way that seems judgmental." Or, "I know that this is an emotional decision to make and I'm not dismissing that at all; I'm simply trying to look outside of those impacts and just focus on the numbers for a moment to help us see this issue from all perspectives." Both of those statements include acknowledging the negative avoiding emotion with the approach emotion of anticipation that gives it the right emotional lift for people listening.

By doing this, you set the stage for others to be authentic too. I learned this many years ago while taking courses from the Center for Ethical Leadership and it's called creating "gracious space." Your framing statement is an invitation for others to feel safe, to be vulnerable, and to share their perspectives as well. This, in turn, helps neutralize the variety of emotions and levels of hyperarousal in the conversation. In a gracious space, because everyone gets to see that everyone else is possibly reacting from a "danger" mode, the collective nervous systems in the room can re-regulate back to safety and to rational thinking.

KNOW WHEN TO ADAPT

Knowing how you will be perceived ahead of time and having a plan to manage that is a social intelligence tactic used by all savvy Shepherds. This is where an aware woman has an opportunity to go into a situation, knowing that she is expected to be warm, empathetic, and collaborative and to make sure that she does in fact meet that expectation and still communicates clearly and directly what she needs to say.

If you aren't aware of the impression you are making with others or what they are expecting, your posture, your tone, and your language can do a lot of harm because as creatures, humans are wired to detect patterns and signs of danger. Therefore, if your body language communicates this danger before you open your mouth, you are toast. Remember what I said in the last chapter, that we make decisions fast and they are usually based on those three key feelings of trust, belonging, or fear. Well, the part of our body that is primarily used to gather this information is the eyes.

So, here is something to remember: smile. Yeah, some women get really pissed when a man tells them how much prettier they would be if they smiled. And those of us with a "Resting Bitch Face" or RBF have gotten sick and tired of this comment, rightfully so.

But as someone who also understands how important it is to manage our impressions, I do have to remind myself to smile in certain circumstances. That is because smiling has a one-two punch for women who are trying to get their point across. One, a smiling face is a safe face. Plus, smiling—even if it's forced—signals the happy neurochemicals like dopamine, endorphins, and serotonin to be released in your own brain.

Yes, believe it or not, once the muscles in your face change to a smile, your brain thinks that something good is happening, so it releases the good stuff. It's like a smile just told your brain, "Hey we're having a party!" and your brain replies, "Cool! I'll bring the wine!" Our brains are weird.

But, weird or not, these neurochemicals then lower your heart rate and relax your body. Yes, even if you are really stressed about what you are about to say and do, forcing a smile on your face will ease that tension and help you remain calm. Plus, it gives the impression to other people that you are confident and can be trusted, even if you really just want to puke.

Smiles also have the same effect on the people we are talking to. If you make eye contact and smile at the other person, they are unconsciously compelled to smile back due to **mirror neurons** in our brains. So, a social intelligence trick used by Shepherds is called **mirroring**, or when we mimic the style of the other person, in body language, posture, volume, and even in the pace and rhythm of the dialogue.

Also known as **limbic synchrony**, mimicking others is a hardwired feature of our brains. Babies begin to demonstrate this when they attempt to mimic our smiles, so it's believed to be an essential part of the learning process. Remember that study done with newborn babies imitating facial expressions I shared a couple of chapters back?

Researchers also theorize that our tendencies to naturally sync up with one another may also be our way of non-verbally communicating with each because it shows we are locked in and connected empathetically.

That's why when you begin to mimic the communication style of the person you are speaking with, you increase the likelihood that not only will you get along, but they will feel that you truly understand their feelings, which can give you the setting to be more persuasive with the points you are trying to make. So, if you are speaking with someone with a more passive style of communication, adapting your messaging to fit with their mannerisms does not mean you become passive and less assertive. It means that you are seeing the conversation from their perspective, shaping the message in the best possible way to match up with their filtering system, like a cat burglar navigating the lasers in the bank vault to get to the motherlode without setting off any alarms.

And if we go back to the power of the smile, due to the mirror neurons, people we smile at receive the same benefits we get when they smile back at us, even if they do not know it. Their own brains release the same happy chemicals, and we can use the power of smile to diffuse tensions in another person and help regulate *their* nervous systems for them. So, a smile really can go a long way to setting the stage to you making your point safely and confidently and reducing the negative backlash to you.

In the end, a Shepherd is always assessing their situation and in full control of the impression or image they want to make while being authentic and true to themselves. A real Shepherd *does* care what others think because they see that it is a critical part of being successful in business. And positivity wins.

BE DIRECT

Have you ever planned out a great conversation in your head only to get flustered later while speaking because of nervousness or lack of confidence? And because of feeling afraid, did you backtrack on what you wanted to say? Or do you tend to talk "around" the point you want to make because you're trying to soften it up? If so, you are not alone.

In fact, researchers find that overall confidence and a fear of speaking go hand in hand. So, a big step in becoming a Shepherd is to first overcome your fear of speaking in front or with others first so that you can then feel confident being direct and holding your boundary.

Finding ways to practice your skills also helps you improve your **verbal fluency**. Verbal fluency is the ability to find the right words to say in a timely fashion. So, if you are someone who gets tongue-tied when flustered or always thinks of the perfect comeback hours after the conversation, you would benefit from practicing your verbal skills. Not everyone needs to be able to get on a stage in front of hundreds or even dozens of people, but Shepherds are able to carry on conversations comfortably and skillfully. You can start to practice at networking events or even with a few friends who also want to practice and build confidence.

However, there are other major changes you can make today to improve your ability to communicate more clearly and directly.

245

Shepherds leave the judgments about the person out of their statements and they don't make them responsible for their feelings. Shepherds instead own their own feelings and talk about the problem, not the person. For example, instead of, "You make me so mad. You are always unprepared for meetings," say, "Sometimes, it appears like there is a lack of preparation for meetings and I feel frustrated because I think you don't care about the work we're doing. What do you think we should do about that?"

Shepherds also don't kneecap their statements. These are the small qualifiers or words women use to "soften" their image and reduce the backlash of being thought of as aggressive. Unfortunately, these kneecaps like, "Excuse me" or "I'm sorry" end up eroding a woman's impression of competency and confidence, hence the term. So, this is a verbal habit from thinking you need to be ready for disapproval that Shepherds learn to break. Instead, switch to statements like, "Thank you for being patient with me" instead of, "I'm sorry I keep asking questions," or drop the kneecap altogether.

Finally, fight the urge to over-explain your reasons for your decisions. Some of us have had to justify our needs for too long and it becomes second nature to validate our positions. But sometimes you really do not need to. It's okay to say what you need or how you feel and leave it at that. If someone attempts to question your reality, consider if it is justified or if they are trying to tell you how you should feel or believe because it suits *their* agenda. When raised in dysfunction, unfortunately, the latter situation was commonplace, but as an adult, you know your reality. You do not need to explain it for someone or argue with their interpretations.

Ultimately, being a Shepherd is about the balance of authenticity, street smarts, and common sense. To be a successful communicator who can express her needs confidently while maintaining a connection with another person is all about being aware and in control of ourselves and our emotional state while being aware of how we appear to others. And a Shepherd does this all while being direct and cooperative. That is why I believe this is a communication approach that best aligns with our programmed tendencies as well as with the expectations that the world has for us women right now, which is to be warm, collaborative, and empathetic.

FINAL STEP TO BECOMING COURAGEOUS: FACE YOUR FEARS

How do we know how courageous we are? Well, according to lecturer, author, and all around inspirational badass Brené Brown, courage is measured by how vulnerable we are.

And that's why I don't expect that after reading this chapter, you will be cured of your insecurities and your confidence will soar. The fact is that the path to courage is a scary trail of doing things that make you feel afraid. And, like many other things we've gone through here, it will take time and practice as well as turning back from danger a couple of times for some of these things to change. But having courage and confidence is non-negotiable for women who want to be successful entrepreneurs.

That is why we keep learning about the power of fear and how it is the driving force behind how we make decisions and choices. So, in becoming courageous, or having the ability to do something that frightens you, step one is facing your fears.

And so, I need *you* to know that when you are afraid today, you are not actually in danger. It's the memory of what could happen when you were small that is triggering those feelings. And this fear undermines your confidence which is your feelings of self-assurance that come from trusting and appreciating your abilities.

See, we think the world is this: a situation arises, then we assess it and determine we cannot do it, therefore we become afraid due to that lack of confidence.

Let's say, for example, you are called upon to stand up at a networking meeting and introduce yourself in front of the whole group. Right away, you get scared and think, "No way!" What is going on inside of your head? Are you worried that everyone will think you're stupid? Are you worried that once you introduce yourself, they will like you less? Are you worried that you will say the wrong thing and stumble on your words? Those thoughts are not based on reality. They are based on subconscious memories from learning to not speak up and stand alone when you were a child.

So, what's really happening is: Situation arises, then **a memory** and fear are triggered, therefore you get a "you can't do this" message from your primal brain to stop you.

And now you falsely believe you lack the skills or competency or whatever to address the situation or say what is on your mind **when there is no actual justification that's even true**. It is all based on a memory your primal brain accessed for reference.

Yes, there are times it's true—you can't do it, whatever that "it" is, like flying a plane perhaps. But there is overwhelming evidence and research that says that most of the time, you are probably wrong and you **can.** I believe you already have all the power to change and you have the skills to do what you want to do, your fearful, protective primal brain is just getting in the way of that.

I know how hard it is to shut off the program in your head that raises your doubts. Been there. Done that. But this brings us to one of the other most important lessons weaved in and out of this entire book: our brains can change. We can, through new experiences, reprogram the script our primal brain is using and feed it new information. We can update the software so that it matches our current, adult situations and stop replaying the program from our childhoods.

If you recall from the discussion earlier, it happens only through the repetitive process of pruning away our old wiring by not doing what we have always done and forming new neurons when we do something different. And then, eventually, and faster than you probably believe it can happen, your primal brain picks up on the changes in your environment, and the alarms begin to quiet in your head and in your body. And the amount of bravery and courage you must sum up decreases as your primal brain learns that it doesn't need to make you feel afraid as often as it thought.

The root of our fears that keep us from speaking up is a fear of being rejected. We all share it. Everyone, dominate or passive, anxious or avoidant, if we cannot speak up and say what we need or how we feel, it's because we're afraid of what will happen to us. Will we be left? Or will we be punished?

As Brené Brown once said, "Vulnerability is hard, and it's scary, and it feels dangerous, but it's not as hard, scary, or dangerous as getting to the end of our lives and having to ask ourselves, 'What if I would've shown up?' 'What if I would've said, *I love you*?' Show up, be seen, answer the call to courage...'cause you're worth it. You're worth being brave."

EXERCISE: WHAT I FEAR MOST

1. When people object to my requests and tell me no, what am I thinking to myself? Do I counter back? If I don't, why don't I ever challenge their refusal? What am I afraid of?

2. Do I speak up in meetings and share my opinions or keep them to myself? Why do I think I do that? What am I afraid of if I say something?

3. What kinds of topics am I sensitive about? Is it my looks? My intelligence? My financial state? Why do I think these subjects bother me?

4. What happens to me or how do I react when forced to talk about or confront one of these sensitive topics? Do

I get angry or defensive? Do I feel ashamed? How do these reactions affect my communication? Do I become a Sheep or a Wolf?

5. What kind of evidence can I find that proves my fears are invalid? Can I think of experiences where I spoke up and got what I asked for or wasn't punished? Do I know other people who have done what I want to do who are successful?

I've spent a great deal of time giving you the context in which they were shaped and how they came to be. Now it's time to draw your fears out and stare at them. Know them. Learn them. Validate them. And sympathize with them. Your fears are from your memories. And your memories are from when you were a child. Let the little girl inside you know that you know why she's afraid. Standing up for herself when she was young did have shitty consequences.

Take the time to be gentle with yourself right now. These fears of yours are real in the sense that they matter. And at some point, they are reflections of valid experiences and how you learned to survive them. But you, my friend, are here to change that and become the woman who can put her hand over her heart when it starts racing and remind that little version of you inside that you've got her now and that she is not in danger anymore.

...

Chapter Seven

BECOMING UNSTOPPABLE

"If women understood and exercised their power, they could remake the world."

—Emily Taft Douglas

It is not lost on me that many of you are reading a book about starting a business in the wake of the biggest economic disaster modern humans have faced worldwide since the Great Depression in the early part of the twentieth century. At that time, nearly 25 percent of Americans were unemployed, and half of the world's banks had completely failed. However, during the worst of the Great Depression, there were only fifteen million without jobs, whereas during the pandemic, the figures were double that. During the early months of the pandemic, the markets crashed, oil prices tumbled and all industries that literally relied on the congregation of groups of people such as retail stores, wedding venues, places of worship, bars and restaurants, and more were all halted indefinitely. The future became very uncertain.

While the world learned invaluable lessons from the Great Depression about stabilizing markets, corporations, and banks as well as during the Recession in the first decade of the millennium, nothing prepared anyone for the pandemic. The old rules didn't apply. And while we all watched the movies and TV shows about zombie apocalypses, never in our wildest imaginations did we ever imagine businesses shutting down everywhere, stay home orders, forced social-distancing practices, and mask wearing.

We were not dealing with overzealous investors creating real estate or tech bubbles that impacted only a few industries terribly and everyone else moderately; we were dealing with a truly life-and-death situation. All of us. Everywhere. As in world-fucking-wide.

When talking about this chapter with a friend, I shared, "I'm trying to figure out how to tell women how they can be just like me and get through hard shit like this in one piece, empowered and with the strength to go on." To which she replied, "Yeah, but Ameé, not to be a downer, that will never happen." Of course, I instantly protested because I believe anything is possible, which meant that I was actually reinforcing her point.

She continued, "If there is one thing I have learned about you and myself, quite frankly, it's that I know that I will overcome whatever problem I have, but I am also always worrying about the 'what if' scenarios. But you, it's like those thoughts never even cross your mind. You just seem completely fearless and push on, and I'm not sure everyone can do that."

And she was right about me. I am that way. Somehow, I have evolved a deep-seated belief in myself that no matter what, I will figure out what to do next and that I will actually be better than I was before.

Replaying her sobering point in my mind, I began to think about how I need to approach this so that I don't mess this chapter up. Because, being a ridiculous optimist, I know anyone can do this. I also know that I'm going to need some evidence to prove it. And you know how much I like to remind you that evidence of the truth is how we learn to put the lies in our heads to rest.

So, I sat at my desk and thought about what do people *really* need to know in order to dust off from a failure or setback in life and in business? And how do I always manage to move forward with the confidence that I will succeed when others in similar circumstances don't?

Because as life just taught us all: your perfectly formatted task lists won't save you once you get punched in the mouth by a disaster. And your five-year plan won't matter if you don't have the energy or will to keep going. And if you really believe that you can't execute on your ideas because it's someone or something else's fault, you will always fail. Period.

And yes, I know that sometimes shit happens that we can't control. But there is always something you *can* control, or do, in every situation that allows you to forge on, even if at first it seems you can't. That is what it means to be unstoppable.

In fact, in this moment I am sitting here at my desk during a pandemic peppered with great social turmoil and unrest, watching a world of grief, fear, and chaos because millions of people are suffering from racial discrimination, economic adversity, and literally being confronted with life-or-death choices. But, even as history has shown us these kinds of events do pass, we can be pretty sure that our future on this planet will come with more and new challenges that will test us in many new and unpredictable ways.

So, I came up with the question I needed to find the answer to: Is my can-do attitude really all that unique and something I just happened to be born with? Or is resilience something that can be taught to people?

And so, I did what I do best: got curious and researched. And I found that no, I am not special. There are, in fact, certain behaviors that not only define what it means to be resilient, but strategies one can employ if they want to train themselves to be more resilient.

WHAT IS RESILIENCE?

Let's start with what researchers have noted in psychology studies: humans have a consistent pattern of thinking about how we view life's inevitable twists and turns. For example, when adversity strikes, we all tend to look backward and try to figure out what went wrong, why it went wrong, and who we can blame. Because, as I've repeated over and over again in this book, the brain learns from experiences.

The Oxford English Dictionary's definition of resilience is the capacity to recover quickly from difficulties. And so, it infers that resilient people do what everyone else does first, but then they do something different—they act.

But how does someone become resilient? That's a great question. Some people seem to be born with it and other aren't. Those with it tend to take it for granted, while those without it struggle with being anxious, depressed, or having feelings of helplessness and powerlessness. And I have seen those with it sometimes show very little grace or compassion for those without as if it is a simple choice to be resilient or not.

Now, when people comment on my mental flexibility and how I have been able to rebuild and reinvent so quickly after adversities like my businesses ending or relationships exploding, I laugh and tell them "Thanks! It's because of all the trauma!"

While I am kidding, it's not actually a lie. But it's not actually all true. Researchers do know that resilience is like everything else we've studied in this book; how much or how little you seem to have of it starts way back during your childhood.

Researchers at the Center on the Developing Child at Harvard University wanted to understand why it is that some children develop resilience and others do not. They found a combination of a biological resistance to adversity and a strong relationship with an important adult in their family or community builds a child's abilities to cope with threats and adversities.

When looking at this supportive adult, the researchers noted that a child **only needed one dependable person** in their life. This person did not have to necessarily be a child's parent. It could have been a relative or teacher or someone from their spiritual or religious community. All that seemed to matter was that this relationship gave a child responsiveness and protection from the disruptions that can come from toxic, sustained levels of stress. These adults also seem to help children develop capacities to plan, monitor, and regulate their own behaviors and understand that they have control over their own behaviors or situations (known as self-efficacy). And these skills, with positive and supportive relationships, all form the foundation of resilience.

So yes, some people are, to some extent, born with the ability to be resilient because of how their brains process serotonin, but it seems pretty important that a child also needs a stabilizing force in the form of an adult who believes and supports them to really give them a fighting chance at learning how to cope with adversity. For me, it was my grandmother, Bette, who protected me, encouraged me, came to support me in everything I did, and sang "You are My Sunshine" and "Zip-a-Dee-Doo-Dah" nearly every day with a warm smile.

Now, the point for you to take from Harvard's research is not that unless you are already resilient, you will never get it. The point is that if you didn't have the experiences and support that would have cultivated it for you as a child, it won't be impossible, but it could be harder for you to develop it as an adult. So please don't judge your results or progress against someone who may have appeared to master it. And, by contrast, if you are a woman reading this who has a cruise ship full of fortitude, I hope you can understand that just like confidence, resilience is truly a privilege, so exercise a little patience and understanding with anyone who may be struggling but is at least trying.

HOW WE ALL HANDLE ADVERSITY

As we have learned, we suffer from our emotions when we don't have any idea of why they are overtaking us and where they are coming from. Our emotions tend to spur on scripts and thoughts in our heads that we think are actually true or real such as that we aren't smart enough or that no one wants to hear what we have to say. These scripts or schemas are our beliefs. When these scripts help us, like the ones that increase our confidence or our courage, awesome! But when these beliefs hurt us and hold us back, these are referred to as self-limiting beliefs.

So, what happens to people who struggle with setbacks or failures and can't move forward? It's usually because they have the scripts locked in, running over and over and over in their heads, and they have no idea that there is a stop button to push. In other words, they are caught in an **emotional trap**. When these thoughts get too out of control, that's when people begin to get anxious, depressed, demotivated, and even procrastinate. Or, conversely, they can be hyper-focused, addictive, compulsive, controlling, or become a perfectionist.

Harvard business and leadership professor Joshua Margolis and one of the world's leading experts on resilience, Dr. Paul G. Stoltz, coauthored an article published in the *Harvard Business Review* in 2010 called "How to Bounce Back from Adversity," noting that most people typically respond one of two ways when something bad happens.

The first is that some people experience **deflation** which is like it sounds—you get the wind knocked out of you. You can either be the type of person who rarely takes risks or someone who has overcome many setbacks in the past. Both types of people can experience deflation. But deflation tends to trap the people who never built up resilience because they simply haven't failed enough times to know that it's a normal part of business or life. Or it can trap those who have intentionally sought out only low-risk activities so that they could build up their win column and collect trophies.

Now, the other emotional trap that people find themselves in after experiencing a setback or adversity is playing the role of a helpless bystander or **victim**. Again, like I said earlier, it's completely normal for humans to try to analyze a bad situation and sort out the what, when, who, and why. The difference is that people with a victim mentality eventually come to the simple conclusion that it wasn't their fault, there is nothing they can do about it, and that's that.

Unfortunately, a victim's biases will keep them from taking accountability for what they did or do have under their control. Plus, if anyone does offer them suggestions or helpful advice for changing their circumstances, they refuse that too. The victim prefers instead to remain focused on the belief that they were right and everyone else is wrong. Or they may instead cling to the belief that nothing they do will matter, and so what's the point?

Martin Seligman, known as the "father of positive psychology," has spent decades studying helplessness and resilience. He was even instrumental in developing a program for the US Army aimed at helping servicemembers cope with PTSD and to mentally protect the men and women of the military against it. What he learned through his years of research and training was that people who don't give up have the habit of interpreting their setbacks or adversities as temporary and changeable. This suggests that in order to immunize a person from giving up after failure, you need to teach them to be an optimist.

But what if optimism isn't your go-to in a situation? Or, like I just mentioned, if you have found yourself trapped by your beliefs due to the overwhelm of the situation? Well, fortunately, there are ways to train you to shift your thinking and to build these skills.

SIX STEPS TO BECOMING UNSTOPPABLE

The basis of we are going to use throughout these several steps is in something I've mentioned before called **cognitive behavioral therapy** or CBT. Used a lot by therapists as well as life or business coaches, CBT describes any type of problem-focused or action-oriented strategy intended to help someone change a distorted thought or behavior they have, as opposed to trying to decipher its meaning.

American psychologist Albert Ellis, claimed by many to be one of the most influential people in the field of psychotherapy, developed the very first CBT technique called Rational Emotive Behavior Therapy back in 1956 with the aim of helping people identify and change their self-harming beliefs so that they could have happier lives.

Most of mindset-shifting strategies coaches use with clients are based on some version of Ellis's **ABCD Model.** These techniques are used to identify the self-defeating or irrational beliefs someone has about an activating event that causes us to become triggered, and then turn those irrational beliefs into rational, self-helping beliefs. Once this is done, then the outcomes, emotions, or consequences will improve.

Research of the effectiveness of the ABCD Model has shown that it has been very successful in raising self-esteem and treating anxiety and depressive episodes. It has also been shown to help people who are prone to rage or anger when triggered because it provides a methodology for dealing and processing with anger, rather than avoiding situations that can trigger it. This is a process that can also be very useful for dealing with fears and self-limiting beliefs someone gets from the thought of speaking up that we just covered in the last chapter.

The ABCD model states that:

Activating events do not cause our emotions, but our self-limiting **beliefs** we have about ourselves cause the

consequences we experience which are the negative emotions we feel and the behaviors or actions we take. Therefore, we must consciously **dispute** our initial self-limiting beliefs and come up with rational, alternative beliefs that probably reflect the truth of what's actually happening. In other words, our circumstances don't have to change for us to see a positive outcome, we need to simply recognize and change our reactions, which I mentioned in the last chapter about understanding our fears.

For example, you can't make a bad business review go away, but after you recover from the very human response of having your feelings hurt, you can choose to change your reaction. This might look like seeing that your customer had a valid complaint, and you can actually make some improvements to your business or services. Or you can see that the review came from someone who you identified as a hater, and it confirms that your branding is working and you can congratulate yourself.

The main things to remember with using these exercises for deactivating our negative, self-harming beliefs and coming up with alternative, constructive beliefs is that we can't stop bad things from happening, but we can control how we respond. And the more positively and proactively with which we approach a bad situation, the more positive the outcomes will be for us, not just in terms of improved mental health, but the positive thinking that can make us more creative. Plus, this positivity is the reserve capacity we need to be resilient. So, it is important we learn how to view adversities as teaching moments. This is why I want to walk you through the steps and exercises you can use to help.

I want to say that there have been countless studies that **this process works and sometimes it works instantly** because a person is able to make a quick link between their thoughts, feelings, and behaviors and see that whatever is happening doesn't actually need to dictate their emotions.

TAKE POSITIVE ACTIONS

While some setbacks can certainly grind you to a dead halt, once the unstoppable entrepreneur has confirmed that they are not dead, they immediately get to finding a way to fire those engines back up and get going again. And to do that, Margolis and Stoltz found through their work that truly resilient people are able to shift from making sense of what just happened to not just positive thoughts, but "now, what am I going to do about it?" action-oriented thinking.

In fact, other experts consistently see in the behaviors of people who are able to rebound from a setback, whether they caused it or not, that instead of getting stuck in the grief of deflation or the blame of being a victim, they do something entirely different. Resilient people look for ways they contributed to the problem or event, then think about whether they had sized it up correctly and if they responded appropriately. And then they wonder what they would do differently if given a second chance so that they can learn from it.

There is a difference here, however, between taking actions that only increase the negativity of the experience or situation, like seeking revenge or adopting self-harming behaviors for coping. Those feel action oriented, like you are gaining some power and control over your situation, but that is not what is meant here. The operative word is "productive," as in you will gain something positive. Revenge or proving you are right might feel positive, but it's really punishment in disguise.

To help people do this in a way that outcomes or actions can be discovered, Margolis and Stoltz identified four lenses to view the event or setback so that you can shift from neutral back into forward movement, and key types of questions to consider. Combined, the questions and observations create a framework that helps a person become resilient in the face of a setback or adversity and address the very normal sense of powerlessness when we are all surprised by a negative experience.

CORE

If you have a hard time seeing the "bright side" of a bad situation, you can do follow this framework to help you review it and come up with some positive actions to help overcome it. For example, in entrepreneurship, finding out that none of your customers are going to pay their bills on time and you are going to have a huge cash shortage on your end, making it hard for you to pay *your* bills, is really tough. Remember that the reason one-third of businesses closed was that they ran out of cash! This is a very real, very stressful scenario that feels like it's out of your control. And one that will beat you up quickly if it happens a few times.

So, when that happens, you can follow this process to sit down and develop an action plan that helps you move from victim to unstoppable by engaging your CORE.

Control—Ignoring the urge to find out why something happened, focus on **what** you can do to improve the situation now. Do this by asking yourself what parts of this situation you can influence that changes its course and which parts are beyond your control.

"I can start calling and emailing my clients who haven't paid me to keep adding some pressure on them to pay their bills. I can also contact my vendors I owe money to and let them know what's happening on my end <u>before</u> they are forced to call me."

Ownership—Ignoring who or what is responsible for the event, identify **how** you can create positive outcomes with your actions immediately.

"If I am able to reach my clients, I can find out their needs and maybe structure a payment plan that gets me some part of their outstanding bill sooner rather than later, which will be helpful to me. Plus, it will show my customers, who are great people going through hard times, I care about them and their hardships. Also, it will help me identify people who might not be good customers for me to have in my business. I can use this experience to identify them earlier."

Reach—Without worrying about the reach this situation will have, identify how to limit the damage. You do this by thinking of ways to minimize the downsides and to maximize the upsides by transforming it into an opportunity.

"I can improve my collection process today by just sending more frequent payment reminders. I am certainly learning how to be more assertive as a result of this and finding myself less afraid to make my calls to my late-paying customers. And I realize that I need to have a buffer in my savings and budgets for times like this, so I don't get caught off-guard again if this happens. Also, I can collect the reasons for the late payments and see if there aren't any external factors I should be aware of that could be seasonal and that will allow me to predict these kinds of events in the future."

Endure—Instead of worrying about how long this situation will last, identify what outcomes you want, regardless, and think of ways to break it down into sections that will allow you to last for the long haul.

"Once this is over, I don't want to be surprised again by not having enough cash to pay my own bills on time. And I will be more knowledgeable about the ups and downs of my business cash flow, so that I can hopefully predict ahead of time and adjust earlier, rather than reacting. For now, I'm going to start with prevention of anymore late payments happening and put extra energy on those with the biggest bills and find ways to get them paying."

When you do this, it is recommended you give yourself fifteen minutes of uninterrupted time to go through, brainstorm, and *write out* your answers to each of the questions. That is because, like anything else, we want to change or improve, repetition is the key to mastery.

Margolis and Stoltz note that just thinking about your situation does not give you the same levels of command and control that committing your answers to paper does. Thinking is good, but it doesn't cement it as well as developing a written plan or strategy for how you are going to proactively move forward.

Resilience is about giving yourself a chance to change your thoughts. So, any time you have any setback or triggering situation, practice these skills. You will find that over time, this type of processing will become second nature, thanks to the wonders of neuroplasticity.

LIMIT CATASTROPHIC THINKING

Even as you improve your resilience, you will still find yourself fearful, because resilience and fear are not independent of one another. If you are afraid, it doesn't mean you aren't resilient. And if you are resilient, well, I guarantee that you will often decide to take actions while terrified. But, when someone is stuck in either analyzing a current setback or trying to prevent one, it is possible that they have fallen into another emotional trap called **catastrophic thinking**.

Anyone of us can fall victim to this at any time. I have had to talk myself off many proverbial ledges of thinking disaster is right around the corner. Contemplating all of the worst-case scenarios is natural and normal. But part of being an unstoppable entrepreneur is not just having an ability to bounce back after a mistake, failure, or adversity, it is also forging ahead into new, uncharted areas without being paralyzed by our fears.

Now, being a pretty bold person myself, I understand that, of course, there is a balance between being foolish and careless with being prudent and tactical. But often, we find ourselves being spooled up by our primal brain working really hard to keep us from doing something and pulling all of those damn alarms again. And that is because once you choose to do something that will move you out of your predictable patterns and comfort zone, it's perfectly normal for your brain to kick into survival mode and start to bring up all the ways it can go wrong.

Sometimes, our uncertainty and fears are because we can't guarantee or predict an outcome and we don't feel comfortable just plunging into the unknown ahead of us. Then we may become trapped by running every "what if" scenario through our heads, hoping that the computer inside of us will spit out some confirmation that everything is going to be okay if we follow a certain path. And just when we think we have a decision; we find a tiny hole or weakness and the process starts all over again. This is catastrophic thinking.

If you haven't learned this yet, you will: the magic in life comes from doing something that will stretch us past our comforts and teach us to grow. So, then it becomes necessary to do things even when you are feeling afraid. Because once you can overcome those fears, you are giving your primal brain new information that is telling it, "Yeah, it turns out that what you thought was dangerous actually isn't." And as you keep feeding your brain your successes, you are teaching that old dog some new tricks and growing your confidence.

I want to give you a framework that I use and recommend for others that will help activate the rational part of the brain where the executive functions live, and invite it into conversation with your primal brain, so that we can get a two-way dialogue happening, like a debate between friends instead of a one-sided freak out session.

TURN YOUR FEARS INTO TO-DOS

Let's use another completely valid scenario: you want to quit your job completely and start your own business. It is a life-changing decision, but you have been uncertain. Now, you just read this book and learned about the piles of other landmines you didn't even expect, and so now, you are really doubting yourself.

But the biggest, nagging fear you have is about your finances and whether you can afford to support yourself as you build your customers and sales up, both justified and reasonable concerns to have.

Step One: Remember why you are doing this. Yes, the very first step in this exercise is to fall in love all over again with your idea or goal by weighing the positives and negatives of choosing to pursue it or to stay on the current course. Go back to your reasons you put down on paper in Chapter Two and reaffirm that, "Fuck yeah! I want this badly!" And if you must, write those reasons down again so that you see them.

Close your eyes, push away the doubts, and just let yourself **feel** the new life: the vacations, the bills paid, the free time—whatever it is you are trying to achieve.

It might seem silly to close our eyes and daydream, but we are using a cool brain-nerd trick here by doing this first in order to get you into the optimum state of mind. How did we do this? Instead of being in a moment of fear and anxiety and having your body producing stress hormones like cortisol, we've got your brain feeding you good chemicals that come from excitement, like dopamine. Remember how forcing a smile makes your brain think you're happy? This is the same thing.

Step Two: List out the worst-case scenarios, one by one. Now, while you put your fears into writing, you might start to feel your anxieties building up again because your primal brain is trying to get back into the discussion. So, it's also important to keep your rational brain in charge by reminding yourself that this is only a to-do list of things you want to plan for.

Example: "What if I don't get __any__ sales for the first year?"

Step Three: Brainstorm all the ways to prevent them from happening. Next, think about this and then brainstorm ways to prevent that from happening, and do your best with keeping it nonchalant and confident.

Example: "Really? No sales? As in zero? Honestly, that's really unlikely if I develop a sales and marketing plan that lets me know every available customer I have and the ways to market to them regularly."

Step Four: Write out your Plan B. Now, you think about what you will do if your worst-case scenario happens.

"If it did happen that I don't get a single sale my first year, it's obvious I would just need to make sure I have saved enough money before I quit my job to cover my major expenses for a year. So, I should make sure as I'm doing my start-up costs, I also write out every business and personal bill I'd have to be able to pay out of my savings and have a separate savings goal just for that. And then when I hit that magic number, I know it's safe to quit my job and go full steam ahead with my business."

Turning your fears into a to-do list is useful for planning anything from what tasks to do in your business to having difficult conversations with other people. I would not expect that you ever stop using something like this, since we are all humans and being afraid is as natural as breathing.

LEARN POST-TRAUMATIC GROWTH

In November 2008, when General George W. Casey, Jr., the Army chief of staff and former commander of the multinational force in Iraq, asked Martin Seligman what positive psychology had to say about soldiers who struggle with PTSD and depression, Seligman explained:

"How human beings react to extreme adversity is normally distributed. On one end are the people who fall apart into PTSD, depression, and even suicide. In the middle are most people, who at first react with symptoms of depression and anxiety but within a month or so are, by physical and psychological measures, back where they were before the trauma. That is resilience. On the other end are people who show post-traumatic growth. They, too, first experience depression and anxiety, often exhibiting full-blown PTSD, but within a year they are better off than they were before the trauma. These are the people of whom Friedrich Nietzsche said, 'That which does not kill us makes us stronger.' "

And so, while learning how to get up after being knocked down is a critical aspect of being successful as an entrepreneur, learning how to grow from it will make you a master. And fortunately, just like we can do things that build our resilience, we can also do things that help us experience **post-traumatic growth.**

When Seligman was tasked with improving the mental well-being of the US Army, he developed a five-module program to teach the soldiers how to not only survive from their experiences, but to grow. I have summarized and paraphrased this for you to read and think about each time you are having an existential crisis with a setback or adverse experience that might impact you and your business.

First, it is important to understand that your response to trauma or failure or adversities, like having a shattered sense of belief about yourself, the future, or anything else, is normal. The overwhelming feelings you feel, such as grief or anger or both, are not a character defect or a sign of a serious condition. But there are ways to reduce the intrusive thoughts and limiting beliefs that will help with reducing your feelings of anxiety. I have showed you a couple already that are based on CBT. They work if you do them. You don't have to feel trapped by your anxiety. You just have to be willing to do the exercises.

The other thing that can limit your abilities to grow from your adversities is bottling up your feelings and keeping them to yourself. That might seem like it's making you "tough," but that can lead to worse outcomes for you. In fact, there are people who will listen, and you need to tell your story, so do it. Try not to let the shame of a voice in your head telling you to "suck it up" or that no one cares about you stop you from finding an outlet. The easiest way to do this is to simply hire yourself a therapist or counselor to listen. If that is not possible, then look for a networking or even a business support group. You can also simply write out everything you're feeling in a notebook or on your computer and include all the ugly things you really want to say or feel. This process allows for the release or ventilation of these emotions, but it's also an opportunity to reexamine the event in ways to help desensitize and normalize it so that you can help prevent long-term negative outcomes.

Seligman also recommends looking on your experience like the Hero's Journey that we talked about earlier in this book. Remember when you were asked to sit down and identify who you are, what you believe in, and then write your own myth? While that is an important exercise for identifying your authentic voice, I hinted to you earlier that it also has some other benefits. That is because it can reframe everything that happened as something that enabled you to find greater appreciation for your strengths as well as deepening your abilities to feel negative emotions like fear, grief, and anger.

In your Hero's Journey, think about what skills you had to summon, what relationships improved, what new doors opened, and how you learned what to truly appreciate in life. Once you have documented and examined your setback and reframed it into a learning experience, you can create a new mantra and identity for yourself with the new principles you have. Just like in Joseph Campbell's *The Hero with a Thousand Faces,* identify the message or purpose you have to share with others as a result of this experience.

In 2011, when Australian runner and engineer Turia Pitt was only twenty-four years old, she was nearly killed during a race. An unexpected grass fire swept up at some point along the ultramarathon course, trapping her and preventing her from escaping. She ended up in the hospital, clinging to life with over 65 percent of her body burned. She would endure losing seven fingers and over two hundred reconstructive surgeries. It would seem that this former model and athlete would never be the same again.

However, what Turia did was turn her overwhelming circumstances into a growth experience. She had to learn how to stand again and then walk. And after that, she started to run again, even fulfilling a dream she'd had of competing in the Ironman Triathlon in 2016. Today, she's a motivational speaker and coach. When asked about her secret recipe for overcoming the immense challenges she had, she credits her growth and resilience to persistence, consistency, and taking small steps each day. In a 2017 article she wrote for BusinessChicks.com, Turia said:

"It's not like I had an epiphany at some point when I turned it around and realized I was going to get through everything. My journey wasn't like that at all."

"But what I did do every day was do the work I had to do. I did my physio sessions. I went to the gym. I did my training sessions. I went to the psychologist. Day in day out I didn't see any changes. I didn't notice any improvements. It was only when I looked back after three months or six months or even a year, I could see it. So, it's not about jumping out of bed, doing a superwoman pose and telling yourself that you're strong and motivated and you're ready to take on every day. It's not that exciting!"

"I think it's more about reminding yourself that things don't happen overnight, committing to the grind, doing the work and taking the small steps that need to be taken every single day. What got me through was applying myself and being really persistent and probably a bit stubborn with it. If I couldn't do something one day, I'd just have to try again the next day."

"Because of what I've been through, I know that I can get through hard times and I know that I'm capable of anything I put my mind to. That's what tough times teach us. Each time I go through a tough time in my life now, I think 'I've had tough times before, and I've survived them—I'm gonna survive this one too.'"

DON'T LET MISTAKES STOP YOU

You don't have to suffer a significant trauma or major event to be knocked down a peg or two. In fact, it's going to be more common that you are going to make bad calls or run-of-the-mill mistakes while you are giving this self-employment thing a go, and those will hurt too. But again, they don't have to define who you are or keep you from sticking with this.

I know for some of you, mistakes came with a heavy price. You've been taught that you should never make them, but whatever you learned, it's not true. Mistakes are the keys to growth, innovation, and building your confidence. Yes—you grow your confidence from trying something new and failing, especially when you can transform that failure into a learning opportunity.

In fact, there is a school of thought in business that preaches to not only fail, but to fail fast! But the truth is, you should fail smart. That is, never stop experimenting and never stop learning.

Now, if you make a mistake that affects other people—and trust me, you will—it will suck and be scary to have to put your tail between your legs, but you have to learn that is also a normal part of business. However, I have seen too many businessowners duck from taking responsibility for their own mistakes and either ignoring their customers or blaming them. It's frustrating and it's a fantastic way to end your business. Given how scary it is to admit we're wrong, can you blame them? No. But can you run a business like that? Also, no.

When I ran my manufacturing company and was creating my groundbreaking recycled-content countertop, trust me, I experimented, failed, and sometimes my customers were negatively impacted by it. But I worked very hard to do a fair investigation on what happened, assigned the responsibility where it belonged (mostly on me), and then made up for it so that the customer got either what they paid for or they were fully reimbursed. And a few times, I financially took it in the shorts, especially if making the situation right for the customer also meant I had to cover a contractor's installation fee. But I always believed that it was a matter of ethics and my personal values to be accountable for our mistakes, even if we didn't mean to make them. I despised the idea of punishing or hurting another person just so I could avoid the discomfort. It earned me a reputation very quickly as being trustworthy, responsive, and reliable.

In fact, when new distributors and dealers wanted to vet me, I gave them the names of several of my existing customers and told them, "Please ask them about all of the times something went wrong." Puzzled, they would ask me why, and I'd say that so many people are always trying to give you their highlight reel. I'd reply, "Because it's easy to do business when everything is going well, but if you want to know what it's really like to work with me, ask them what I'm like when business goes bad."

So, what is my magic formula for handling mistakes as a business owner?

First, own it. Don't run from it. Don't deflect it. Own the mistake and do it quickly. The longer you wait to acknowledge you messed up, the longer you allow your customer to sit with their own anger and disappointment and the whole situation festers. Want to know how to get business-killing bad reviews? Make a mistake and then ignore the offended party. That will do it every time. But if you find out there's a problem, even if you don't have an answer, don't ignore your customers email or phone call—take it, gather information, let them know you're going to figure it out. And then apologize and validate their discomfort. The sooner you can calm their nervous system down, the better the outcomes will be for everyone.

Now fix it. Figure out the remedy for the situation and stand by it. And accept the fact that mistakes are costly, so be prepared to pay whatever it takes. This is why understanding your risks in your business early are important so that you can set aside a little money in a savings account to cover warranty or performance claims and get business insurance to cover for them so that a mistake doesn't close down your business. But try to avoid being cheap—it leaves a bad taste in your customers' mouth. I recommend that you do the "Fears into To-Dos" exercise to brainstorm several worst-case customer scenarios so that you can actually have a plan before the first call comes in. It will help you be prepared as well as be a tad desensitized to it.

Don't do it again. I was willing to fix my mistakes quickly and fully because I could always tell myself, "Well, now we know that we are going to make sure that **never** happens again!" After an error or mistake was made, I always reviewed it from every angle and figured out how to prevent it in the future. Sometimes, mistakes are from bad materials or a faulty process for making something. But sometimes, mistakes stem from misunderstandings, so corrective actions can include looking at wording on your website or marketing materials as well as making sure your products are made better. Mistakes are common and to be expected, but repeating the same one is a sign of something much worse. If your customers keep having the same problems over and over again, it's not that they are "dumb," it's because you are. So, stop it.

Don't quit. Again, there is nothing as heart-sinking and gut-twisting as finding out something is wrong. Talk about triggering childhood trauma—wow! Being scolded by a teacher or parent is one of the worst feelings any of us have ever experienced. Dealing with their anger, or worse, their disappointment—ugh. So, yeah, your confidence gets shook when you make a mistake. And yeah, those nasty self-limiting beliefs get stirred up really quickly and you think, "Fuck it. I'm done. I can't do this anymore." But come on, ladies—are you really going to quit over one little mistake? No, of course not. So, get back out there and keep at it.

BUILD YOUR RELATIONSHIPS

Finally, if the biggest factor for developing resilience as a child was the presence of a secure and caring adult, then it goes without saying that if you are trying to do this as an adult, you need the same thing.

Eventually, your internal power cell will work fully on its own, but even then, it never hurts to have people around you to remind you of what a rock star you are. That's why the most important relationships for developing the mental toughness and mental flexibility you need to preserve are positive ones. It's not bullshit. According to Seligman, even the US Army found that changing the leadership qualities of training sergeants from the prototypical degrading, screaming caricature we are used to seeing in movies to those who offer more frequent and constructive praise resulted in the men and women in their commands flourishing.

In fact, when I spoke with Dr. Ronda Beaman, a resilience expert and business coach, she said the very **first step to building resilience** is to take note of who your circle includes and to make sure you have people around you who reinforce the belief that you are worth it. Before you can become resilient and unstoppable, you must believe **you deserve to be powerful**. As Ronda said, "Make sure that the hands you are holding are of people who feed your heart and make you feel that you are important."

So, if you have people who can be critical, but not critics, and who can tell you what you need to hear so that you can improve, that is gold. And if you don't have anyone close by, then find examples or models of people who inspire you in books or on YouTube and let them show you the evidence that you can overcome and achieve your dreams.

Turia Pitt echoed this, saying that her emotional support crew got her through her darkest days. But, when she needed an extra lift, she would intentionally read the inspirational stories of other men and women who overcame life-changing events.

You have seen me mention many times in this book that your herd can hurt you or they help you, so it is important you are building yourself a go-to network of freedom-hungry, profit-seeking, badass Pollyannas who are all going to help one another crush their respective goals. And seriously, when it comes to starting a great business just like other successful entrepreneurs who are living the life of their dreams, why can't that also be you?

• • •

Chapter Eight

BECOMING THE FUTURE YOU

> *"Doing the best at this moment puts you in the best place for the next moment."*

—Oprah Winfrey

As this book concludes, I want to take us back to the beginning with this question: Why do want to go into business for yourself? Because if there is one single thing that will always inspire you to pick yourself up off the ground, dust yourself off, and keep going, it's to never forget why you are doing all of this to begin with. The best way to get in touch with our big reason "why" is to remember to ask ourselves the following questions any time we stumble or doubt ourselves:

- What do I want?
- Why do I want it?
- What do I need to do to get it?

Now, imagine if you had a crystal ball and could look just twelve months ahead and talk to yourself then. Who is that woman and what is she like? She's not imaginary. This isn't fiction. This is you. But are you the same? Or did you start to do some of the things in this book I strongly suggested? Because if you did, you are definitely going to be different. But in what ways? How? What did you decide to start doing right away? And then, I want you to imagine that you are offering advice to your past self, which is you today. What would we tell our former selves if we could?

And let's take this a little further. Maybe you know what you *want*, but do you know what you are going to **have to change** in your environment and within yourself to be that person twelve months from today who will enjoy this future when you get there? I ask you this because too many entrepreneurs focus on the business side of starting a business and never get the breakdown like you have about all the inner world work that also has to happen in order to actually be successful, present company included. And so, their overall business goals lack the self-improvement and personal development that are also fundamental to success.

You see, it's relatively easy to create a business that looks successful to everyone else out in the world but, in fact, is bankrupt. Entrepreneurs are prone to use misguided measurements for what a "successful" business is by comparing the image of the business against other people. The problem is that these comparisons are masking the cancer growing inside themselves that leads to self-sabotage. For example, your business could be getting sales, but are *you* making money?

And when I learned all that, I knew that I had to stop being a fool. That meant realizing the reason I never became the

Future Me I had so desperately and vividly imagined was because I wasn't yet the woman who could be her. Not even close. And then it was no wonder nothing turned out the way I wanted. I was focused on the wrong things. I weighed myself and my abilities against false metrics that led me to believe I was a success when, yeah, I have been good at the business stuff, but I was terrible at the taking care of myself stuff which, guess what, ended up ruining my business stuff.

Here's the secret no one ever told me that I'm telling you: the least risky but yet most impactful thing you can do to prepare yourself for starting a business is, quite honestly, doing the things that make you a savvy and emotionally and socially intelligent businesswoman. Seriously. It will hardly cost you anything. In fact, unless you hire a coach or a therapist, it will only cost your time and your efforts to put into practice many of the things I've talked about. And that is an investment in something that will never be taken away from you. Ever.

Now, I want you to think about everything in this book and start to identify all of the things you need to change or begin to develop in yourself and your life that are preparing you for the future waiting for you. I want you to be ready for the moment your dream shows up on your doorstep and says, "I'm here, Bitch! Now, get in car and let's go!" Because when that time comes, you won't have time to pack your bags, say your goodbyes, and take off. No, you *need* to be ready because your dream reveals itself to you in opportunities that you have to be able to recognize and seize.

Also, think about this: do you need to wait twelve months to be her? Nope. True, you will have to make some changes, which we are going to get to. But you know, here's a crazy thought—I bet you don't even have to wait six months before you can start enjoying some of the of the things you thought you'd have to wait a full year for. Often, we dream and imagine and fantasize about what we will be and how much cooler life is *going* to be, and we stop appreciating how cool life is right now!

So, instead, I want you to think about right now and the shifts and change you can make **today** that don't hinge on you getting your business started so that you can start to experience this new life you really want for yourself. Because happiness doesn't come from owning your own business. It comes from within.

EXERCISE

1. **My Entrepreneurship Skills.** What areas do I see that I could start working on improving right now? Where can I learn more?
2. **My Herd.** Do I have people around me who are positive and supportive? Where can I meet other people who are? Are there mentors or other people who are living the life I want who I can learn more from about their habits, behaviors, and practices?
3. **My Mental Game.** Have I seen some areas in my confidence, emotional intelligence, or self-awareness that I can start to improve today? Can I practice my social intelligence skills by becoming more observant and understanding of others and their inner worlds?

4. **My Environment.** Am I living in the right town or state to do what I really want? Does my workspace allow me to focus? Am I surrounded by things that inspire me or do they demotivate me?

Now, look at this list and think about these things as you decide which ones to start right now so that you can become your Future You. Are there small changes you can make right now that would make you happier? And of all the changes you can make, which ones are the easiest that you can do all on your own?

Finally, I want you to choose three to five specific changes you can make immediately, so that you can begin to experience the journey toward your destination right away.

UNCOVERING YOUR FUEL LEAKS

Since again, unstoppable is about motion, let's think about the car we've been driving toward our destination. What happens when the car runs out of gas? It stops. It doesn't matter how great the car is or how fast the car is, no car runs on an empty tank. And that goes for the driver too, which is you. If you are asleep at the wheel, disaster awaits. If you aren't focused on the road, you can get sidetracked. If you don't like where you are heading, you won't even bother to turn the key.

Now, something to note is that if we have grown up with dysfunction, we are really good at running on a low tank of gas. There is no rest during survival. And yet, this "hustler" mindset is what is thought to be a major character feature of the successful entrepreneur. The truth is, however, that successful businesswomen know that's not the case. It's not the quantity of the hours you put into your business—it's the quality.

Don't get me wrong, some days, yes, I grind. I wake up at four o'clock, work for four hours writing or podcasting, switch over to coaching and consulting for another eight hours, and then the next thing you know, I've just dropped a twelve to thirteen hour day, fueled by ten cups of coffee and one microwave burrito. But I have learned to place limits that I respect for my own well-being as well as for my family. And so, those days are not the norm.

But even when I am in grind-mode for a long period of time, no matter what, I get a full night's sleep. That is non-negotiable. And to do that, I stop with the mental work no later than five o'clock and I don't exercise after six o'clock in the evening. Years ago, I also stopped having a nightly glass of wine or two, and I am in bed at such an early hour that my social life changed completely. No more late dinners or hanging out and drinking with friends. I let people know that I turn into a pumpkin by nine o'clock, so when I do get together with friends, I'm the Happy Hour Gal, leaving me time to be home to make dinner for my kids, get to bed on time, and be up early the next morning seven days a week. And to be honest, knowing what I want and why I want it makes it really easy to say "no" to things that keep me from getting there.

Over the past couple of years, I also learned a lot about how I recharge myself too. I identified the work I did that made me feel fulfilled and what kinds of tasks made me feel like I was poking my eyes out. And I discovered, after scaling back on socializing, how much of an introvert I really am. I was in survival mode for so long, I never slowed down long enough to give that side of myself time to breath.

In the course of a couple of years of part trial and error as well as intention and accidents, I shifted from a person who couldn't sit still and needed to literally be physically moving or doing something seven days a week to someone far more balanced. I'm not slower, per se, but instead I'm more like a pendulum, with a graceful consistent arc that goes from one end to the other, in perpetual motion.

When I know I need to work hard, I know I also need to rest hard. When I know I have to do things I don't love, I make sure it's balanced with something I do. And I don't burn myself out—if there is a demanding project or task I have to do, instead of putting my head down and not coming up for air for days or weeks, I make a point to refill every day so that my tank is full the next morning.

While much of what I learned came from observations, I also found out much of these important things from my own personality tests. While the tests talk about how you are and how you appear to others, the real benefit is that understanding your drive helps you identify the fuel tanks that you need to monitor.

First, a lot of women make choices to start a home-based business without fully realizing the impacts that working in relative isolation has on a person's motivation or mental energy. Stay-at-home orders certainly raised this awareness for many people. How oriented we are toward our outer world versus our inner world is a place where we can have our energy sapped. This trait is the one called **extraversion** from the Big Five I mentioned earlier in the book.

A person high in extraversion gets their energy fuel tank refilled from being around other people. So, if you are naturally sociable, outgoing, and love to connect with others, being a solopreneur will drain you after a while. This is where coworking spaces are a great option for extroverts—if you are disciplined enough to get your work completed and don't spend too much time chatting with everyone all day.

On the other hand, people who are low on extraversion, called introverts, have their energy levels refilled in quiet isolation, where they are given time to process their inner world, thoughts, and feelings. As a solopreneur, working alone is great. However, working around a lot of people or having a lot of social interactions during the day, like in a customer service setting, will dry up their tanks fast.

So, when this tank is low, an unaware entrepreneur will start to get distracted by things like checking in with the friends on social media to get their fix if they are extroverted. Or they will start avoiding the phone calls they need to return and spend too much time on a solo project if they are introverted. In either case, due to a low fuel tank, we sub-consciously find ways to refill it that are not always conducive to our business objectives and may be self-sabotaging. And then, again, if we don't know what's really happening, we punish and shame ourselves for our lack of focus and discipline.

That's why, whether you are an extrovert, introvert, or ambivert like me who is right in the middle, if you don't have the time to get away and refill yourself, it will begin to affect your productivity, concentration, and motivation. So, whether it's joining networking groups so that you can hang out with lots of people or locking yourself in your bedroom to meditate, or a bit of both, structuring it into your routines is key.

Now, another energy killer that we can find our personality tests is in our traits that feature thoughtfulness, impulse control, and goal-directed behaviors. The Big Five calls this **conscientiousness**. This spectrum includes people on the high end who tend be organized, plan ahead, and dislike constantly changing situations or unexpected deadlines, as well as those on the low end who reject structure and might procrastinate on detail-oriented tasks.

The problem with running your own business, as I've outlined earlier, is that all the work involved is a combination of big picture and details. You must be able to do both. My personality, for example, is very low on this factor. This makes me really good in ambiguous situations that would scare people who are high in this area. But it also makes me terrible at a job that has the same tasks to do day after day.

Just like with how we adapt for our extroversion traits, we can also experience distraction, procrastination, and demotivation if we find ourselves constantly doing work that isn't what we are naturally comfortable doing. So, people high in conscientiousness stress out when the unexpected pops up and may tend to avoid taking care of it. Or they tend to be reactive instead of proactive, waiting for clear direction instead of brainstorming solutions. People low in this factor love to do big vision planning but will let the mundane details, like paying bills on time, get lost. In both cases, the unaware entrepreneur is procrastinating on the things they know they must do but can't figure out why they lack the drive to do them.

An added danger that I have seen take down the best micro businesses is that a businessowner will see that there are parts of the job they hate or feel incapable of doing, and so they hire it all out on day one, before they have actually figured out whether they have the financial resources to do so! Then, they find themselves in cash crunches that turn into hurt feelings because they can't pay the bill to their bookkeeper or office assistant, for example.

For combating these issues, I found that reframing the nature of work we hate into realizing that it's necessary to get what we love is hugely important. In other words, by using CBT again, all you have to do is change the way you describe the tasks to yourself by shifting them from negative to positive in order to help you develop different feelings about them.

For example, when I have to do a task that is time-consuming and requires little to no thinking, instead of thinking of how boring it is, I view it as a great way to shut my brain down and recharge. I put on headphones, music, and tell people to not interrupt me so that I can get it done quickly.

Finally, there is one more major area of energy awareness that I have discovered makes a huge difference on your effectiveness and that is really beginning to understand your **mental rhythms** throughout the day. While we have all been trained to regard the business day as somewhere between eight and five o'clock, the reality is that our brains are not all structured to operate at Level Ten for that length of time or even *during* that time of the day.

For example, once I started waking up at five o'clock on a regular basis so that I could be up ahead of my kids to help them get ready for their 6:15 a.m. school bus, I noticed how sharp and creative I was early in the mornings. I started to find that I could knock off a full day's worth of work before ten o'clock. So, then I started to wake up at five o'clock even on the weekends to see what was up. It was consistent, so I leaned into it.

I began to make sure that the work that needed my full, focused attention would get attacked right when I woke up. When I did that, I no longer had a long list of incomplete tasks wearing me down all day. Then, I started to note my mental energy levels dropped around three o'clock every day. At that time, I found that it was harder to focus and do things like writing. But, strangely enough, I could still look at data and numbers.

So, I shifted again, and I made sure to put on my afternoon plate the tasks that weren't impacted by the dips in mental energy. And if I didn't have work that needed to be done at all, three o'clock was the perfect time for me to go to the gym. Coincidently, three o'clock was also when my kids were coming home from school and I needed to be on "Mom Duty," which was hard to do when I had unfinished work. So, by realizing how to work smarter and in sync with my mental energy, I created a win-win: I got my work done and then could be more emotionally and physically available for my family.

The other downside of the set business day is that the peak mental energy that you want to allocate on complex tasks might overlap with someone wanting to call and talk to you about something else. This then breaks your focus and robs you of your best work. Once I realized this for myself, I began to get pretty protective of my peak times and set some boundaries to prevent being **time-sharked** by others. I don't take calls, answer texts, or respond to emails until I am ready to shift gears. Otherwise, I find myself becoming frustrated and then my emotional energy tanks start dropping. Of course, like everything, balance is key and so is mental flexibility. So, I plan ahead for interruptions and either choose to table what I'm doing until the next morning or find a way to recover quickly so that I can stay on track.

As a result of these discoveries, now I know that the best way to tackle a big project that will require my peak mental energy is to wake up earlier rather than to stay up later. But for some people, their rhythms may be the opposite, so instead of assuming that your brain may work in the same way, I advise that you find out your best times of the day to get things done.

To do that, start to pay attention each day to when you seem to be able to get work done efficiently and effortlessly. Also, notice when it seems to take you longer or you become easily distracted. Take note of the time of day and what is going on. You will start to notice a pattern in the work you do and when you do it best. This will allow you start to rearrange your to-do lists to match your mental rhythms, and you will see your effectiveness improve.

REFILLING THE TANKS

While I highlighted major areas where we expend our energy in business, it's important to know where the tanks or reservoirs actually exist. And by knowing that, we then know how to check in to make sure they are filled and how to pump fuel in when they need to be topped off.

The Energy Project, founded by Tony Schwartz, has been looking at how organizations and businesses can help their people become aware of their energy levels and to maximize their well-being as well as their output. Through their work and research, they have identified four dimensions to our personal energy which are **physical, emotional, mental,** and **spiritual**. Just like I learned through experience, they have found that the key is to make sure that we don't wait until we burn every last drop before we pull into the gas station. The key is to consistently be spending and refilling in order to maximize the positive outcomes.

Now, again, as I mentioned at the beginning of this section, those of us who have learned to operate in survival mode for so long pride ourselves for being able to make due with very little. We view our abilities to be workaholics as a badge of honor. But it isn't sustainable. Even if it looks like it's been working for you for so long, the reality is that, yes, you have some success at being a hustler, but your results are limited and could be so much more once you learn to change.

Think of it this way: we all learned how to operate a car that runs on gas and that operating it involved pushing the pedal to the floor and racing ahead until it stopped. But what if instead of learning how to stop for gas before the needle hits "E," you actually learned how to swap out the engine for a power cell that constantly recharged itself? Can you not see how advantageous it would be to not have to pull over and stop for gas all the time? Not having to stop and start over and over again is literally what it means to be unstoppable.

So how do we refill our four tanks or keep them topped off while trying to live our regular life and start a new business? The Energy Project recommends adopting a few of these practices:

Body or Physical Energy: Taking care of your body is the backbone of all of your other energy tanks, and yet many of us (present company included) can let it run dry. Without performing the necessary routine maintenance on our physical form, we lack the resources to handle emotions and other mental tasks well. So, to keep your physical energy levels renewed, you must:

- Improve your sleep by going to bed earlier and reducing alcohol use.
- Exercise regularly, ideally at least three times a week.
- Don't let your body go hungry by eating small meals or light snacks throughout the day.
- Learn to see when your body is running down, like yawning or difficulty concentrating.

Emotional Energy: It should come as no surprise to you by now why I have spent a great deal of time talking about and understanding emotions in this business book. And that is because when we are in control of our emotions, instead of our emotions controlling us, we can improve our lives and our positive outcomes tremendously. So, these are simple rituals for helping to keep our positive emotional energy renewed:

- When you are triggered, try to diffuse your negative emotions like fear, anger, or impatience through slow, deep abdominal breathing. This technique is like mini-meditation and buys you time so that you can re-regulate your fight-or-flight system back to zero.
- Keep positive energy high by making it a consistent point to express your gratitude and appreciation for others. Believe it or not, telling others how much you appreciate them has benefits to them as well as to you, and so this is a particularly powerful ritual.
- Use the tips from the last chapter and keep your positive energy levels high by reframing upsetting situations as opportunities for gaining new understanding or learning.

Mental Energy: This goes back to the discussion about knowing your mental rhythms and then adopting some additional practices that take advantage of your natural settings to minimize disruptions that can be costly and demotivating:

- Reduce the likelihood of interruptions when doing high-concentration work by putting your phone or emails away.
- Set up designated times for answering emails and returning phone calls. Believe it or not, you don't have to answer everything as soon as it comes in!

Spiritual Energy: This is not about religion or belief in a higher power; this is about your authenticity and sense of purpose. While I gave you ways to ensure that as you establish your business, you spend time defining what those values are, it is important to be reminded how to replenish yourself and reorient back toward them when you feel adrift:

- Using your personality tests as an aid as well as your own feelings, identify the work that fills your soul and make sure you are doing it.
- Identify your priorities, whether they are people or activities, and build in time every day to spend on them. And then defend that time like your life depended on it, because in a way, it does.
- Know who you are, what you stand for, and unapologetically live that way. Don't let the opinions of others stop you or make you feel like you have to compromise on what you believe is important and define who you really are.

298

LAYING OUT THE ROUTE FOR THE JOURNEY

Finally, you can't start a trip toward becoming the Future You without a little bit of a plan in mind. Now, I will be completely honest: my planning is a blend of shit stuck in my head, stuff I jotted down in a notebook once, and spreadsheets with fifteen tabs. I have my bigger visions written in a notebook somewhere here in my house, but I don't reference them very often because once I wrote it down that one time and then closed my eyes, I cemented it into my brain. Personally, I don't need to have my destination in outline format that I update daily to know what I want and what I am working toward. But the details of what the next year looks like, you bet I have that broken down for myself on what I need to be doing.

You now know what business skills you probably need to learn and develop. And, you have probably identified some personal and self-improvement work you need to tackle and what changes to your lifestyle, network and environment that probably needs to happen to. So with all of that, you can now start to layout out a route on your map and begin to assign some milestones you need to achieve in a logical order that will take you from your starting point today out to your destination five years from now or whenever you thought it would be.

What is good about this exercise of working backward from your goal is that it can help reveal to you whether your goal is truly achievable in the timeframe you want it to be. Some people—check that—**most** people set unrealistic deadlines on their goals because they are swept up by the urgency from thinking that this new business will solve all of their problems **right now**. It's that good old desire to have **instant gratification**. And so, they jump in that car and start driving, hoping that they will just arrive one day to where they want to be.

Sadly, most people never do. And do you know what happens when you don't achieve your goal in the time you expected to? Your confidence is shot. You may believe that you are a failure and that you shouldn't have even done this to begin with. And the reality is that you are truly capable of doing it, you just got a little too aggressive and set yourself up for failure.

So, sustaining success comes from also being patient and deliberate, which is hard for some of us that were born to hustle and move fast. Also, starting without a little planning means you are setting yourself up to have your outcomes determined by your experiences and forcing you to adjust to them rather than dictate them on your terms. So, zeal is good, Grasshopper, but so is composure and diligence.

EXERCISE

1. **Long-Term:** What is your ultimate destination and when are you going to be there? Is it five years from now, for example?
2. **Mid-Term:** How do you know you reached the half-way point? What are the objectives, goals, and skills you

need to have earned, achieved, or developed by the half-way mark or in 2.5 years from now?

3. **Near-Term:** Now, thinking about the next twelve to eighteen months, what do you need to be working on and have completed or achieved so that you are half-way to half-way, or 25–30 percent of your entire journey?

4. **Monthly Targets:** What does each month look like for the next twelve to eighteen months so that you are on track? What are you starting and completing before you begin the next steps and how will all these link together to get you to where you need to be in order to sit down one year from now and plan out the next twelve to eighteen months?

Now, my other secret here is that not only do I lay out a route, but just like I do on a real road trip, I routinely check in with the progress. First, I look out long-term on the horizon and make sure that, yep, I am still heading in the correct direction—even though I can't see it specifically, I know the destination is out there in front of me. I then put my head down just a little and review the route out ahead of places I haven't gotten to yet but will and make sure that yes, it still seems like the right way to go. Or sometimes I will ask myself, "Am I making good time here? Am I ahead of schedule and if so, would I do something a little differently now?" like maybe moving up some relocation plans or expansion for the business. And then I look around me in the present and near-term by checking my spreadsheet and some of the tasks I have there.

In the end, while resilience is our ability to get up and keep going after setbacks, having solid planning skills helps us understand in which direction we need to keep heading. And planning, when paired with resilience, helps us feel that in the Wild West that is the world of entrepreneurship, there are things that we can and do have control over. So, keeping your eye on the horizon and that vision of your future self in your heart will fuel you through the toughest days. And you too will be unstoppable.

...

Conclusion

LAST CALL

The several seconds of lingering silence after I finish is finally broken by our server, "Do you all want anything else? We're getting ready to close."

I turn to her and then shift my eyes down toward my sweaty glass that has collected a pool of condensation around it on the table. That's when I realize that, with all of the talking I've been doing, I have been nursing the same diluted margarita all night.

The last few women who have stayed throughout the evening all look to be trying to come out of the listening trance and shift gears for a moment, so I speak up, "No, I think we're good. We're done here too."

Looking back to you, still sitting on the lounge sofa in front of me, I know what I have to do next.

This is where I remind everyone to remember to breath. I know I just shared some heavy, heavy stuff, and you are going to need a minute. So, it's okay to take some time to think about it all. Being an entrepreneur is not an easy thing to do, so you should sit here first and appreciate that you have taken a very important step in starting, even if you haven't picked out a business name yet.

And I want to remind you that this wasn't all about trying to convince you of problems that you may or may not have in your life. I'm not trying to stir up shit where it doesn't belong. But you looked right at me and asked me to tell you what you really needed to know to start a business, and I did. And I would bet that a lot of it was not what you were expecting.

But trust me, it was what you needed.

First, I wanted you think about why you want to have your own business to begin with and help you uncover some of the beliefs we have about what being self-employed can do for us. I then wanted you to imagine what being self-employed can *really* do for you and why you should focus on that instead. Because if you don't have a big reason for "why" you are doing this, you haven't given yourself the most important key to keeping you going when the route gets rocky and tough.

While I am not trying to create a feminist manifesto, I did want to tell you the dirty secrets people don't or won't talk about when it comes to why women are disadvantaged in ways men aren't when it comes to not just entrepreneurship, but our professional lives in general. So, throughout this book, I also wanted to point out to you how the game is rigged against women in business and how it came to be. But, most importantly, I wanted to show you how you can now recognize when it's happening and make the changes in yourself so that you can succeed. Because if you keep walking into the same traps and hazards that keep women from being paid their real value, you risk never achieving the financial freedoms you deserve.

And I know I took some hard shots at hobby-style businesses or side hustles, but not because I don't think they can be great money-making endeavors but because I wanted to push you out of thinking small. You deserve to think bigger and better!

My ultimate goal here was to tell you the **truth** about why some people succeed and others don't in entrepreneurship, including myself, and I didn't want to sugarcoat any of it. Like I said in the Introduction—once you decided that you wanted to start your own business, well, you and I just became friends. And not only that, but I also just joined your herd, and I'm going to be that girlfriend who is always going to tell what you **need** to hear, not what you **want** to hear. And I wish I had known earlier in my career and life all of these things I just told you.

This book isn't meant to be read once and then forgotten. Nor is it meant for you to do all of the exercises in a weekend. Some of the things I covered will get you thinking right away, and others will be tools for your tool chest to pull out later when you are ready or when you need them. Remember, there are things you can start doing today that can actually change your life without having to start your business quite yet.

So, as you arrive here at the end, maybe a bit breathless and a tad overwhelmed, here is what I don't want you to do: I don't want you to think that none of what I just said applies to you and your business because you are playing small by choice and aren't aiming for "life-changing freedom," that all you wanted to do was to just have a side hustle and make some extra money and who cares if it's not perfect. It's good enough for you. And I know that you will look around at your friends and your beliefs and think that they aren't worth changing because generally everything appears to be fine. Or all of this just feels like it's too much to do right now. Those are the biases in your head convinced they are protecting you. And it's okay—we all have them.

Hear me out, then—instead of putting this book back on the shelf and powering ahead, following the status quo, I want you to just spend awhile observing and verifying everything I wrote about. Start your business the way you thought you needed to. Do the things your friends tell you to do. Follow the lead of other people but keep an open mind and watch what happens, to you, your business, and the others around you. Test what I've said. It's okay. I don't mind the challenge. I just want you to be better.

With that said, if you decide after all this is said and done to not start or restart your business, I hope you at least try to gain a greater sense of control and awareness of your life and well-being. I know it is hard to be the first in your family or circle to stretch out for something bigger than anyone else you know ever wanted. It's scary in fact and can be lonely for a while. But there is a lot value in being the first one who breaks the cycle, not just for you, but for everyone after you.

And so, if you come away from this all a *little more* courageous, a *little more* authentic and doing your best to not let the world stop you anymore, then you are braver than you know—more fearless than you ever imagined.

And I am so proud of you.

XOXO

AFTERWORD

When you picked up this book, you were thinking about starting your own business. But as Ameé has shown you, this is really about starting your most authentic life.

Ameé's message is clear: in order to succeed, keep learning about yourself. She wants you to succeed not only financially, but as a genuine person in a life you have crafted as your own. In fact, she cares about this so much, she keeps reminding you that in order for your business to be sustainable, your self-awareness has to be exquisite.

I can't think of a more enjoyable way to ensure your continued success than to dip back into this book every time you need a refresher on some aspect of your self-creation process. More than most, you now have a roadmap into what will promote your dreams and—just as importantly—what might hold you back. The next step is all yours. By now, you understand that knowing yourself and handling realities are both essential for a successful business and a meaningful life. You've just had a crash course not just in entrepreneurship, but in truth itself.

Now with Ameé by your side, you're ready to get to it! Your freedom is waiting.

Lindsay C. Gibson, PsyD
Clinical Psychologist and author of *Adult Children of Emotionally Immature Parents*

• • •

ACKNOWLEDGEMENTS

Books are never written alone, so here's where I get to say thank you to a few people.

First, I have to say thank you to fellow author and psychologist Dr. Elizabeth Cohen for making the introduction to Mango Publishing. This was life-changing for me as I got a chance to connect with my editor, Jane Kinney Denning, who has been tremendously supportive and encouraging throughout the entire process from proposal to creating the final manuscript and beyond. And this goes to all of the smart and sharp people at Mango, who have done their best through the worst of times and have no easy feat of publishing a business book while the world is dealing with a historic economic contraction. When it comes to publishing a book, honestly, the writing is easy. What they have to do is hard. So, thank you!

I also have to say thank you to two very important women who are, in many ways, the inspiration behind this book, which is why I tapped them to be my draft readers. First is Katrina Cooper, my childhood friend that I've known since we were fifteen. If you must know, she is my jewelry maker that I speak to in this book—the one I want to see succeed so badly. She followed along with the progress of the book as I was writing it, giving me her feedback and impressions. I knew that in the end, if I couldn't connect with her, then I wasn't going to write anything worthwhile for anyone else, so her input was so important to me.

And the second woman is my best friend, Sharon St. Marie. We have shouldered many ups and downs together in our business and personal lives over the last several years, and when I say in this book to go get yourself a good herd of unstoppable, badass businesswomen, she's who I mean. She also read the manuscript while I was writing it and provided me with insight and bucketloads of encouragement along the way.

I also have to say thank you again to Lindsay Gibson. When I decided to take the next leap toward writing this book, she too offered support as well as some great tactical advice. I'm proud to also have her in my herd. She is the example, I hope, for you all to not be afraid of reaching high when looking for mentors to help you along the way. If you would have told me when I first read her books that she'd be writing the Afterword for my own book less than three years later, I would have asked you what you were smoking at that time.

I need to throw in a shout-out to Sarah Gilbert from Transitions Therapy in Connecticut for her review of my opening statement about womxn. I am a human with good intentions and always learning how to turn them into actions. From day one, I knew that I had to speak to gender and to make certain that this book was inclusive to all. So that's why I decided to have a statement right off the bat. And even though I have personal experience with trans and non-binary people, I really didn't want to stick my foot in my mouth because I didn't want to hurt anyone unintentionally. So, I asked Sarah to help make sure that didn't happen.

In this book, you have also read examples of women in entrepreneurship. For the most part, I have not used their real names for privacy reasons. However, there are two exceptions. One is Elizabeth Lambert, a personal coach in the Seattle who shared with me the story of her personal relationships. I want to thank you for your openness and candor and giving me the chance to share your wisdom with the readers. The second one is a woman I met many years ago while we were both in the wedding industry, and she is Anna Gordon, who is self-employed in direct sales with Monat and traveling the US with her family. I knew she needed to have a place in this book because she too represents the possibilities for most of us when we are ready and willing to throw out all the expectations others have for us and just do what we want.

Finally, writing is a muscle that needs to be exercised often. And the more you do it, the better you get at it. So, honestly, I can't sit here and not acknowledge one of the most important facets in the creation of this book and that is all the writing between me and my friend, Brian Ellefson. What started out innocently as just keeping each other up to date through email burst into a wildfire of inspiration. The more I wrote, the sharper and more pronounced my writing skills turned. We joke that our word count between us started to tip heavily in my direction with every email. And at one point, I realized I needed a different outlet because he was having a hard time keeping up with the replies!

But I refer to him as my Merlin in my dedication because what happened is truly magical. Over the course of just a couple of months, my passion for writing came alive again, and he kept the fires stoked, adding fuel where necessary, either through humor or love. So, when I finally decided it was time for me to take that next step toward getting a book going, he was the first person I told. He is and always will be a charter member of the herd I started gathering around me as my life underwent its dramatic transformations. His pride in me is invaluable as well as his unwavering belief in what he is so certain I will achieve. And he knows that I appreciate him for that. I just wanted you to know that too.

APPENDIX A: A LIST OF PSYCHOMETRIC TESTS

The following links are to the current most widely used psychometric tests. Some of the tests can be sampled free of charge while others will give you more robust results at a nominal cost. This list may not include every option available and this is not an endorsement for any test or company.

Predictive Index: Predictive Index is primarily offered to organizations, but they do have a sample assessment option: www.predictiveindex.com.

Truity Psychometrics LLC (www.truity.com) offers free and paid versions of DiSC, Myers-Briggs, and Enneagram.

Myers-Briggs from MBTI has a complete assessment with explanations and guidance for under fifty dollars: www.mbtionline.com/en-US/Products/For-you.

The Enneagram Institute: The test is a newer option in the field of psychometrics and is also known as the Riso-Hudson Enneagram Type Indicator. This site allows you to take the test and provides you with a report for less than twenty dollars: www.enneagraminstitute.com.

16Personalities is another option for the individual to gain insights into personal behaviors. They call theirs the NERIS Type Explorer, but it still based on the same theories as the other assessments: www.16personalities.com.

To learn more about your attachment style and its influences on your personality, you can take this test:

www.psychologytoday.com/us/tests/relationships/
relationship-attachment-style-test.

REFERENCES

"4 Types of Communication Styles," Alvernia University, accessed April 17, 2020, online.alvernia.edu/articles/4-types-communication-styles.

"A Report on Women's Business Ownership," Institute for Women's Policy Research, 2018, accessed March 30, 2020, iwpr.org/wp-content/uploads/2018/07/C472_Report-Innovation-and-Entrepreneurship-9.4.18.pdf.

"AAP Says Spanking Harms Children," American Academy of Pediatrics, accessed March 8, 2020, www.aap.org/en-us/about-the-aap/aap-press-room/Pages/AAP-Says-Spanking-Harms-Children.aspx.

"Albert Ellis," Wikipedia, accessed April 26, 2020, en.wikipedia.org/wiki/Albert_Ellis.

"Being Assertive: Reduce Stress, Communicate Better," Mayo Clinic, accessed April 10, 2020, www.mayoclinic.org/healthy-lifestyle/stress-management/in-depth/assertive/art-20044644.

"Building an Etsy Economy: The New Face of Creative Entrepreneurship," Etsy, accessed March 29, 2020, blog.etsy.com/au/files/2016/01/Building-an-Etsy-Economy-The-New-Face-of-Entrepreneurship-AUSTRALIA-FINAL.pdf.

"Celebrating Creative Entrepreneurship Around the Globe," Etsy.com, Spring 2019, extfiles.etsy.com/advocacy/Etsy_GlobalSellerCensus_4.2019.pdf.

"Codependency," Wikipedia, accessed April 18, 2020, en.wikipedia.org/wiki/Codependency.

"Cognitive Bias," Wikipedia, accessed April 8, 2020, en.wikipedia.org/wiki/Cognitive_bias#List_of_biases.

"Cognitive Dissonance," Psychology Today, accessed March 26, 2020, www.psychologytoday.com/us/basics/cognitive-dissonance.

"Common Family Roles in Addictive and Codependent Families," accessed December 5, 2019, www.recoveredfamily.com/codependency/codependencyandfamilyroles.aspx.

"Content Analysis," Columbia University, accessed March 21, 2020, www.mailman.columbia.edu/research/population-health-methods/content-analysis.

"Definition of Executive Function," American Psychology Association, accessed March 8, 2020, dictionary.apa.org/executive-functions.

"DSM-5 Changes: Implications for Child Serious Emotional Disturbance," DSM-5 Child Mental Disorder Classification, Substance Abuse and Mental Health Services Administration, last edited June 3, 2016, www.ncbi.nlm.nih.gov/books/NBK519712.

"Emotional Intelligence," Wikipedia, accessed April 13, 2020, en.wikipedia.org/wiki/Emotional_intelligence.

"Executive Function & Self-Regulation," Center on the Developing Child, Harvard University, accessed March 3, 2020, developingchild.harvard.edu/science/key-concepts/executivefunction.

"Fact Sheet: Women & Socioeconomic Status," American Psychological Association, accessed March 30, 2020, www.apa.org/pi/ses/resources/publications/women.

"Frequently asked questions about earnings data from the Current Population Survey (CPS)," US Bureau of Labor Statistics, accessed March 15, 2020, www.bls.gov/cps/earnings-faqs.htm.

"Frequently Asked Questions About Small Business," US Small Business Administration Office of Advocacy, September 2019, cdn.advocacy.sba.gov/wp-content/uploads/2019/09/24153946/Frequently-Asked-Questions-Small-Business-2019-1.pdf.

"Gender Bias at Work: The Assertiveness Double Bind," Culture Plus Consulting Pty. Ltd., accessed April 10, 2020, cultureplusconsulting.com/2018/03/10/gender-bias-work-assertiveness-double-bind.

"Gender Identity & Roles: Feminine Traits & Stereotypes" Planned Parenthood, accessed March 30, 2020, www.plannedparenthood.

org/learn/gender-identity/sex-gender-identity/what-are-gender-roles-and-stereotypes.

"Gender Role," Wikipedia, accessed March 30, 2020, en.wikipedia.org/wiki/Gender_role.

"Gender Stereotyping," Office of the United Nations High Commissioner for Human Rights, accessed March 30, 2020, www.ohchr.org/EN/Issues/Women/WRGS/Pages/GenderStereotypes.aspx.

"Highlights of Women's Earnings in 2018," US Bureau of Labor Statistics, Report 1083, November 2019, www.bls.gov/opub/reports/womens-earnings/2018/home.htm.

"History and Mission," Center for Applications of Psychological Type, accessed March 14, 2020, www.capt.org/about-capt/history-mission.htm.

"How Women Undermine Themselves with Words," Goop.com, accessed April 24, 2020, goop.com/wellness/career-money/how-women-undermine-themselves-with-words.

"John Bowlby," Wikipedia, accessed April 21, 2020, en.wikipedia.org/wiki/John_Bowlby.

"Joshua D. Margolis," Harvard Business School, accessed April 26, 2020, www.hbs.edu/faculty/Pages/print-profile.aspx?facId=10658.

"Labor Force Statistics from the Current Population Survey," US Bureau of Labor Statistics, accessed March 15, 2020, www.bls.gov/cps/cpsaat39.htm.

"Myers-Briggs Type Indicator," Wikipedia, accessed March 21, 2020, en.wikipedia.org/wiki/Myers–Briggs_Type_Indicator.

"New Study: Women Judged More Harshly When Speaking Up Assertively," press release, VitalSmarts, August 5, 2015, www.vitalsmarts.com/press/2015/08/new-study-women-judged-more-harshly-when-speaking-up-assertively.

"One Simple Skill to Curb Unconscious Gender Bias," VitalSmarts, August 4, 2015, www.vitalsmarts.com/crucialskills/2015/08/one-simple-skill-to-curb-unconscious-gender-bias.

"Paul G. Stoltz, PhD," PEAK Learning, accessed April 26, 2020, www.peaklearning.com/dr-paul-g-stoltz.

"Pink-Collar Worker," Wikipedia, accessed March 27, 2020, en.wikipedia.org/wiki/Pink-collar_worker.

"Positive Psychology Exercises" from the Positive Psychology Toolkit, PositivePsychology.com, accessed April 26, 2020, positivepsychology.com/

"Poverty Facts: The Population of Poverty USA," Poverty USA, accessed March 15, 2020, www.povertyusa.org/facts.

"Relationship Attachment Style Test," PsychTests AIM Inc, 2020, testyourself.psychtests.com/testid/2859.

"Resilience," Center on the Developing Child at Harvard University, accessed on March 3, 2020, developingchild.harvard.edu/science/key-concepts/resilience.

"Serve and Return," Center on the Developing Child, Harvard University, accessed June 18, 2019, developingchild.harvard.edu/science/key-concepts/serve-and-return.

"Social Intelligence," Wikipedia, accessed April 25, 2020, en.wikipedia.org/wiki/Social_intelligence.

"Tabula Rasa," Encyclopedia Britannica, published November 6, 2016, www.britannica.com/topic/tabula-rasa.

"The Four Basic Styles of Communication," UK Violence Intervention and Prevention Center, www.uky.edu/hr/sites/www.uky.edu.hr/files/wellness/images/Confl4_FourCommStyles.pdf.

"The Top 20 Reasons Startups Fail," CB Insights, last updated November 6, 2019, www.cbinsights.com/research/startup-failure-reasons-top.

"Toxic Stress," Center on the Developing Child, Harvard University, accessed March 3, 2020, developingchild.harvard.edu/science/key-concepts/toxic-stress.

"What Are ACEs? And How Do They Relate to Toxic Stress?," Center on the Developing Child, Harvard University, accessed March 3, 2020, developingchild.harvard.edu/resources/aces-and-toxic-stress-frequently-asked-questions.

"What is Verbal Fluency?" Art of Verbal War, accessed April 24, 2020, artofverbalwar.podia.com/courses/verbalfluency/60849-introduction/173110-what-is-verbal-fluency.

"Women and Finances," America Saves, accessed March 30, 2020, americasaves.org/organizations/downloads-and-resources/partner-resource-packets/women-and-finances.

Ackerman, Courtney E., "What is Self-Confidence?" Positive Psychology, accessed April 11, 2020, positivepsychology.com/self-confidence.

Allianze Women, Money, and Power Study, "For Women, rising social power is not coinciding with a rise in financial confidence," Allianze Life Insurance Company of North America, accessed March 30, 2020, www.allianzlife.com/-/media/files/allianz/pdfs/newsroom/2019-women-money-and-power-summary-sheet.pdf.

Anchor, Shawn, "Positive Intelligence," Harvard Business Review, January-February 2012, Harvard University.

Bachleda, Amelia, "What You Need to Know About Neuroscience," Interview by Ameé Quiriconi, *One Broken Mom*, February 2, 2019, audio, 1:00.52, podcast.ameequiriconi.com/109574/942122-1-34-what-you-need-to-know-about-neuroscience.

Beaman, Ronda, "How To Harness Adversity with Dr. Ronda Beaman," Interview by Ameé Quiriconi, *One Broken Mom*, August 1, 2020, audio, 1:00.12, podcast.ameequiriconi.com/109574/4811135-how-to-harness-adversity-with-dr-ronda-beaman.

Becker-Phelps, Leslie. "Is Your Attachment Style at the Root of Your Struggles?" *Psychology Today*, September 30, 2019, accessed April 20, 2020, www.psychologytoday.com/us/blog/making-change/201909/is-your-attachment-style-the-root-your-struggles.

Behary, Wendy, "Our Ego at Work with Wendy Behary," Interview by Ameé Quiriconi, *One Broken Mom*, May 24, 2020, audio, 1:18.26, podcast.ameequiriconi.com/109574/3893255-our-ego-at-work-with-wendy-behary.

Brescoll, Victoria L., and Eric Luis Uhlmann. "Can an Angry Woman Get Ahead?: Status Conferral, Gender, and Expression of Emotion in the Workplace." *Psychological Science* 19, no. 3 (March 2008): 268–75. doi:10.1111/j.1467-9280.2008.02079.x.

Brogaard, Berit. "12 Ways to Spot a Female Misogynist," *Psychology Today*, August 12, 2019, www.psychologytoday.com/us/blog/the-mysteries-love/201908/12-ways-spot-female-misogynist.

Brown, Brené. "The Call to Courage," Netflix, 2019.

Bucher-Koenen, Tabea, Annamaria Lusardi, Rob J. M. Alessie, and Maarten C. J. van Rooij, "How Financially Literate are Women? An Overview and New Insights," Global Financial Literacy Excellence Center, WP 2016-1, February 2019, accessed March 30, 2020, doi.org/10.1111/joca.12121.

Campbell, Joseph. *The Hero with a Thousand Faces*, third edition, Joseph Campbell Foundation, (1949) 2008.

Caprino, Kathy, "The Top 6 Communication Challenges Professional Women Face," *Forbes*, December 6, 2012, www.forbes.com/sites/kathycaprino/2012/12/06/the-top-6-communication-challenges-professional-women-face/#69fff2d54f00.

Carlin, Barbara A., et al. "Bridging the gender gap in confidence," *Business Horizons*, 61, Issue 5 (September-October 2018): 765-774, doi.org/10.1016/j.bushor.2018.05.006.

Cherry, Kendra. "The Big Five Personality Traits," accessed March 14, 2020, www.verywellmind.com/the-big-five-personality-dimensions-2795422.

Constable, Simon, "Women, Especially, Are Failing Financial Literacy," *Wall Street Journal*, June 14, 2015, www.wsj.com/articles/women-especially-are-failing--inancial-literacy-1434129899.

Currie, Lara, "How to Have Difficult Conversations with Lara Currie," Interview by Ameé Quiriconi, *One Broken Mom*, January 11, 2020, audio, 53:29, podcast.ameequiriconi.com/109574/2460332-how-to-have-difficult-conversations-with-lara-currie.

Dalla-Camina, Megan, "The Reality of Imposter Syndrome," *Psychology Today*, accessed November 11. 2020, www.psychologytoday.com/us/blog/real-women/201809/the-reality-imposter-syndrome.

Ekins, Emily, "What Americans Think About Poverty, Wealth, and Work: Findings from the Cato Institute 2019 Welfare, Work, and Wealth National Survey," Cato Institute, September 24, 2019, www.cato.org/publications/survey-reports/what-americans-think-about-poverty-wealth-work.

Eurich, Tasha. "What Self-Awareness Really Is (and How to Cultivate It)," *Harvard Business Review*, accessed December 5, 2019, hbr.org/2018/01/what-self-awareness-really-is-and-how-to-cultivate-it.

Fraley, R. Chris. "Adult Attachment Theory and Research: A Brief Overview," accessed December 9, 2019, labs.psychology.illinois.edu/~rcfraley/attachment.htm.

Gallo, Amy. "How to Be Assertive (Without Losing Yourself)," *Harvard Business Review*, August 21, 2012, hbr.org/2012/08/how-to-be-assertive-without-lo.

George, Bill. Authentic Leadership: Rediscovering the Secrets to Creating Lasting Value, Jossey-Bass, 2004.

Gibson, Lindsay C. *Adult Children of Emotionally Immature Parents: How to Heal from Distant, Rejecting, or Self-Involved Parents*, New Harbinger Publications, Inc., 2015.

Gibson, Lindsay C. *Recovering from Emotionally Immature Parents: Practical Tools to Establish Boundaries & Reclaim Your Emotional Authority*, New Harbinger Publications, Inc., 2019.

Gluckman, Pratima Rao, "When Women are Called 'Aggressive' at Work," adapted from Nevertheless, She Persisted: True Stories of Women Leaders in Tech, Next Avenue, accessed April 10, 2020, www.nextavenue.org/working-women-called-aggressive.

Gordon, Anna, email to Ameé Quiriconi, December 15, 2019

Graham, J. Alan, "Relationships: The Anxious Style," Atlanta Center for Couple Therapy, accessed April 20, 2020, www.

atlantacenterforcoupletherapy.com/relationships-the-anxious-style.

Graham, J. Alan, "Relationships: The Avoidant Style," Atlanta Center for Couple Therapy, accessed April 20, 2020, www.atlantacenterforcoupletherapy.com/relationships-the-avoidant-style.

Hanks, Julie de Azevedo. *The Assertiveness Guide for Women: How to Communicate Your Needs, Set Healthy Boundaries & Transform Your Relationships*, New Harbinger Publications, 2016.

Hardy, Karen, "Turia Pitt: 'We need to teach our children about resilience,'" *The Sydney Morning Herald*, May 16, 2018, accessed July 19. 2020, www.smh.com.au/lifestyle/life-and-relationships/turia-pitt-we-need-to-teach-our-children-about-resilience-20180510-p4zehj.html.

Hendriksen, Ellen, "Nine Ways to Fight Imposter Syndrome," *Psychology Today*, accessed November 11. 2020, www.psychologytoday.com/us/blog/how-be-yourself/201708/nine-ways-fight-impostor-syndrome.

Henry Ford Quotes, The Henry Ford, www.thehenryford.org/collections-and-research/digital-resources/popular-topics/henry-ford-quotes.

Hougaard, Rasmus, Jacqueline Carter, and Marissa Afton. "Self-Awareness Can Help Leaders More Than an MBA Can," *Harvard Business Review*, January 12, 2018, hbr.org/2018/01/self-awareness-can-help-leaders-more-than-an-mba-can.

Iacoboni, Marco. "Mental Mirrors" adapted from *Mirroring People: The New Science of How We Connect with People*, Macmillian, accessed April 11, 2020, www.naturalhistorymag.com/features/28883/mental-mirrors.

Kerr, Michael E. "One Family's Story: A Primer on Bowen Theory." The Bowen Center for the Study of the Family. 2000. www.thebowencenter.org.

Klontz, Brad and Ted Klontz. *Mind over Money: Overcoming the Money Disorders That Threaten Our Financial Health*, Broadway Books, 2009.

Klontz, Brad, "Why Women Don't Know Their Worth," Interview by Ameé Quiriconi, *One Broken Mom*, June 1, 2019, audio, 48:45, podcast. ameequiriconi.com/109574/1223168-why-women-don-t-know-their-financial-worth-with-dr-brad-klontz.

Kuntze, Jeroen, Henk T. van der Molen, Marise Ph. Born. "Big Five Personality Traits and Assertiveness do not Affect Mastery of Communication Skills," *Health Professions Education*, Vol. 2, Issue 1 (June 2016): 33-43, doi.org/10.1016/j.hpe.2016.01.009.

Lambert, Elizabeth, Interview by Ameé Quiriconi, February 28, 2020.

Laurie T. O'Brien, Brenda N. Major & Patricia N. Gilbert, "Gender Differences in Entitlement: The Role of System-Justifying Beliefs," *Basic and Applied Social Psychology*, 2012, 34:2, 136-145, DOI: 10.1080/01973533.2012.655630, dx.doi.org/10.1080/01973533.2012.655630.

Maloney, Mary E, and Patricia Moore. "From aggressive to assertive." *International journal of women's dermatology* vol. 6,1 46-49. 7 Nov. 2019, doi:10.1016/j.ijwd.2019.09.006.

Margolis, Joshua D., and Paul G. Stoltz. "How to Bounce Back from Adversity." *Harvard Business Review* 88, nos. 1/2 (January–February 2010).

Maxfield, David. "How to Avoid Social Backlash in the Workplace," VitalSmarts, accessed April 11, 2020, www.vitalsmarts.com/crucialskills/2015/08/how-to-avoid-social-backlash-in-the-workplace.

McDougall P, Vaillancourt T. Long-term adult outcomes of peer victimization in childhood and adolescence: Pathways to adjustment and maladjustment. Am Psychol. 2015;70(4):300-310. doi:10.1037/a0039174, pubmed.ncbi.nlm.nih.gov/25961311.

McGinn, Kathleen L, Mayra Ruiz Castro, and Elizabeth Long Lingo. "Learning from Mum: Cross-National Evidence Linking

Maternal Employment and Adult Children's Outcomes." Work, Employment and Society 33, no. 3 (June 2019): 374–400. doi:10.1177/0950017018760167.

McLeod, Saul, "Cognitive Behavioral Therapy," Simply Psychology, accessed April 26, 2020, www.simplypsychology.org/cognitive-therapy.html.

McLeod, Saul, "Cognitive Dissonance," Simply Psychology, accessed March 26, 2020, simplypsychology.org/cognitive-dissonance.html.

Meinert, Dori, "What Do Personality Tests Really Reveal?" SHRM, accessed March 14, 2020, www.shrm.org/hr-today/news/hr-magazine/pages/0615-personality-tests.aspx.

Menand, Louis. "What Personality Tests Really Deliver," The New Yorker, accessed March 21, 2020, www.newyorker.com/magazine/2018/09/10/what-personality-tests-really-deliver.

Morin, Christophe, Patrick Renvoise. The Persuasion Code: How Neuromarketing Can Help You Persuade Anyone, Anywhere, Anytime, John Wiley & Sons, 2018.

Napikoski, Linda, "What is a Pink-Collar Ghetto?" ThoughtCo., March 18, 2017, www.thoughtco.com/pink-collar-ghetto-meaning-3530822.

O'Connor, H. & Gibson, Nancy. (2003). A Step-By-Step Guide to Qualitative Data Analysis. Pimatisiwin: A Journal of Aboriginal and Indigenous Community Health. 1. 63-90.

Olekalns, Mara, Ruchi Sinha, Carol T. Kulik. "3 Of the Most Common Challenges Women Face in Negotiations," Harvard Business Review, September 30, 2019, hbr.org/2019/09/3-of-the-most-common-challenges-women-face-in-negotiations.

Park, Gregory et al. "Women are Warmer but No Less Assertive than Men: Gender and Language on Facebook." PloS one vol. 11,5 e0155885. 25 May. 2016, doi:10.1371/journal.pone.0155885

Piper, Michelle, "Broken Moms: The Narcissistic Mom," Interview by Ameé Quiriconi, One Broken Mom, July 17, 2018, audio, 41:55, podcast.ameequiriconi.com/109574/753574-1-9-broken-moms-the-narcissistic-mom.

Pitt, Turia, "The powerful lesson I want to teach my son," September 1, 2017, accessed July 19, 2020, businesschicks.com/turia-pitt-truvee.

Reynolds, Marcia, "The Fine Art of Female Assertiveness: How to get your way by being diplomatically assertive," *Psychology Today*, accessed April 10, 2020, www.psychologytoday.com/us/blog/wander-woman/201011/the-fine-art-female-assertiveness.

Riggio, Ronald E., "The Dangerous Art of Impression Management: How to balance authenticity, tact, and common sense," *Psychology Today*, accessed April 24, 2020, www.psychologytoday.com/us/blog/cutting-edge-leadership/201310/the-dangerous-art-impression-management.

Riggio, Ronald E., "There's Magic in Your Smile: How smiling affects your brain," *Psychology Today*, accessed April 24, 2020, www.psychologytoday.com/us/blog/cutting-edge-leadership/201206/there-s-magic-in-your-smile.

Riggio, Ronald E., "What is Social Intelligence? Why Does it Matter?" *Psychology Today*, accessed April 12, 2020, www.psychologytoday.com/us/blog/cutting-edge-leadership/201407/what-is-social-intelligence-why-does-it-matter.

Rigoglioso, Marguerite, "Researchers: How Woman Can Succeed in the Workplace," Stanford Business, March 2, 2011, www.gsb.stanford.edu/insights/researchers-how-women-can-succeed-workplace.

Rivera, Joeel, and Natalie Rivera, "Life Coach Training," Transformation Academy Inc, (Worksheets received November 2019), transformationacademy.com/life-coach-training.

Robert F. Anda et al. "Childhood Abuse, Household Dysfunction, and Indicators of Impaired Adult Worker Performance," *The Permanente Journal* Vol. 8, No. 1 (Winter 2004): 30-38.

Schwartz, Tony and Catherine McCarthy, "Manage Your Energy, Not Your Time," *Harvard Business Review*, October 2007, Harvard University.

Selva, Joaquin, "Albert Ellis' ABC Model in the Cognitive Behavioral Therapy Spotlight," PositivePsychology.com, accessed April 26, 2020, positivepsychology.com/albert-ellis-abc-model-rebt-cbt.

Shorey, Hal. "Come Here, Go Away: The Dynamics of Fearful Attachment," *Psychology Today*, accessed April 20, 2020, www.psychologytoday.com/us/blog/the-freedom-change/201505/come-here-go-away-the-dynamics-fearful-attachment.

Silvestrini, Elaine, "Women & Financial Literacy," Annuity, accessed March 30, 2020, www.annuity.org/financial-literacy/women/.

Soeiro, Loren, "What Does it Mean to Have an Insecure Attachment Style?" *Psychology Today*, accessed April 20, 2020, www.psychologytoday.com/us/blog/i-hear-you/202001/what-does-it-mean-have-insecure-attachment-style.

Stanny, Barbara. *Secrets of Six-Figure Women: Surprising Strategies to Up Your Earnings and Change Your Life*, Harper Business, 2004.

Stone, Pamela, and Meg Lovejoy. "Fast-Track Women and the 'Choice' to Stay Home," The Annals of the American Academy, 596 (November 2004): 62-83, journals.sagepub.com/doi/10.1177/0002716204268552.

Tartakovsky, Margarta, "Catastrophic Thinking: When Your Mind Clings to Worst-Case Scenarios," PsychCentral, accessed April 26, 2020, psychcentral.com/blog/catastrophic-thinking-when-your-mind-clings-to-worst-case-scenarios.

Tatkin, Stan. *Wired for Love: How Understanding Your Partner's Brain and Attachment Style Can Help You Defuse Conflict and Build a Secure Relationship*, New Harbinger Publications, 2012.

Webb, Jonice. *Running on Empty: Overcome Your Childhood Emotional Neglect*, Morgan James Publishing, 2014.

Weir, K. "The lasting impact of neglect," *Monitor on Psychology*, 45(6), June 2014, www.apa.org/monitor/2014/06/neglect.

Weisberg Yanna, DeYoung Colin, Hirsh Jacob, "Gender Differences in Personality across the Ten Aspects of the Big Five," *Frontiers in*

Psychology, Vol. 2 (2011), 178, www.frontiersin.org/article/10.3389/fpsyg.2011.00178.

Wittenberg-Cox, Avivah. "If You Can't Find a Spouse Who Supports Your Career, Stay Single," *Harvard Business Review*, October 24, 2017, hbr.org/2017/10/if-you-cant-find-a-spouse-who-supports-your-career-stay-single.

Young, Jeffrey E., "Schema Theory," Jeffrey Young, PhD., accessed March 22, 2020, www.schematherapy.com/id30.htm.

• • •

ABOUT THE AUTHOR

Ameé is an entrepreneur and businesswoman with nearly two decades at the helm of many organizations—from small home-based businesses to multi-million-dollar companies. In her professional career, she has worked in a variety of seemingly unrelated fields, from construction to manufacturing and weddings to healthcare, gaining incredible experience in each field while earning real successes.

But it's not her achievements that make her a valued and knowledgeable teacher. It's her failures. After one such personal failing, she took time to solve the mystery of being cursed with great ideas and at the same time unable to realize their full potential. During a two-year period, she discovered that she was the architect behind her self-sabotage. That was also the moment she realized her true purpose in life.

Today, through her work in the fields of psychology and self-improvement, she brings a thought-provoking harmony of practical strategies together with the underlying drives that affect women and their business success. She loves to write, coach, and teach. However, when she's not so intensely focused on helping women change their lives, she enjoys spending time with her kids and closest friends. And anytime she can get away, you're likely to find her outside somewhere sunny, with earbuds in and punk music playing.

Mango Publishing, established in 2014, publishes an eclectic list of books by diverse authors—both new and established voices—on topics ranging from business, personal growth, women's empowerment, LGBTQ studies, health, and spirituality to history, popular culture, time management, decluttering, lifestyle, mental wellness, aging, and sustainable living. We were recently named 2019 *and* 2020's #1 fastest growing independent publisher by *Publishers Weekly*. Our success is driven by our main goal, which is to publish high quality books that will entertain readers as well as make a positive difference in their lives.

Our readers are our most important resource; we value your input, suggestions, and ideas. We'd love to hear from you—after all, we are publishing books for you!

Please stay in touch with us and follow us at:

Facebook: Mango Publishing

Twitter: @MangoPublishing

Instagram: @MangoPublishing

LinkedIn: Mango Publishing

Pinterest: Mango Publishing

Newsletter: mangopublishinggroup.com/newsletter

Join us on Mango's journey to reinvent publishing, one book at a time.